Church Growth—
A Mighty River

D1566864

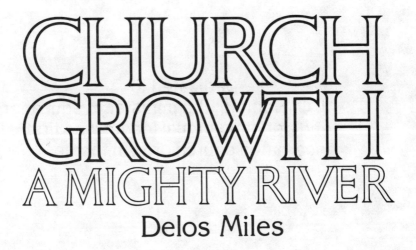

CHURCH GROWTH
A MIGHTY RIVER

Delos Miles

BROADMAN PRESS
Nashville, Tennessee

Dedicated to
J. C. Hatfield, the minister of education
and denominational leader who first
incarnated church growth for me

4262-27
ISBN: 0-8054-6227-9

Scripture quotations in this publication are from the Revised Standard Version
of the Bible, copyrighted 1946, 1952, © 1971, 1973 by the National Council of
the Churches of Christ in the U.S.A., and used by permission.

Dewey Decimal Classification: 270.82
Subject heading: CHURCH GROWTH MOVEMENT
Library of Congress Catalog Card Number: 80-67352
Printed in the United States of America

Preface

The river motif is used to build this basic introduction on church growth. A great river such as the Mississippi or the Nile offers numerous analogies for church growth. Church growth is indeed a mighty river which, like "the river of the water of life" (Rev. 22:1), waters the tree of life and results in the healing of the nations.

I do not know if the genesis of this book was my conversion at the age of eleven, my call to preach at the age of seventeen, my graduation from seminary at the age of twenty-four, or my entrance into the classroom full time at the age of forty-four. Most likely, the volume grows out of all these milestones in my pilgrimage and everything else in between, preceding and following them.

If it is true that we are a part of all that we have met, then, my view of church growth has been shaped by my experience as a Southern Baptist Christian and churchman. Therefore, I thankfully and freely acknowledge that my offering is made from the perspective of one Southern Baptist who feels good about his denomination.

You will readily see that from start to finish I take the church growth movement very seriously. One of my goals is to enter into an honest dialogue with the leaders of the church growth movement. Another is to introduce the large body of literature on church growth. I hope the notes on each chapter will point the reader to those books and articles and other resources which will enable him or her to master the subject.

While the chapters are intended to flow together into a wholistic unity, for the most part they may also stand alone. Accordingly, there is some intentional repetition and overlapping in content. Moreover, the longer I teach, the more I become convinced that planned repetition is an aid to learning.

Contents

1. Its Headwaters and Fountainhead

Peter Wagner estimates that 55,000 persons become Christians every day, and 1,400 Christian churches are planted every week around the world.[1] Yet, there are more than 2.7 billion who have not responded to the gospel, with over 100 million of them here in America. These statistics reveal what church growth is all about, for church growth means "all that is involved in bringing men and women who do not have a personal relationship to Jesus Christ into fellowship with Him and into responsible church membership."[2]

This idea of bringing men and women into a personal relationship with Jesus Christ and into responsible church membership is certainly not new to us. Christians have been doing that under such headings as missions, evangelism, and religious education for a long time. The new thing here is that term "church growth." From whence does it come and what does it mean?

It is at this point that the analogy of a river begins to help us. If we think of church growth as a river, and can locate the fountainhead and headwaters of that river, we shall begin to understand where church growth comes from and something about the nature of its waters.

The fountainhead and headwaters of the church growth river are to be found in a man, an institute, a bulletin, a school, and a book.[3]

The Man

The man is Donald Anderson McGavran, the son of missionary parents, born in India on December 15, 1897, who was himself a third-generation missionary in India for more than thirty years under appointment of the United Christian Missionary Society (Disciples of Christ). He has a Ph.D. in education from Columbia University. McGavran is commonly considered the father of the church growth movement. He began to use the term "church growth" because he was disgusted with the way more liberal churchmen were interpreting the older and more familiar terms of "missions" and "evangelism."

While McGavran has written no autobiography and no one has attempted to write his biography, three portraits of him have been shared in *God, Man and Church Growth.*[4] One of those portraits is by United Methodist Bishop J. Waskom Pickett.[5] Pickett's book, *Christian Mass Movements in India,* which appeared in the early 1930s, was summarized and commended at the 1938 International Missionary Council meeting in Tambaram.[6] Evidently, McGavran was very positively impressed with Pickett's study.[7] Later, in 1936, McGavran collaborated with Bishop Pickett, A. L. Warnshuis, and G. H. Singh in a study which has undergone five editions and is now titled *Church Growth and Group Conversion.* [8]

A second, and more revealing, of those portraits is by A. R. Tippett, a colleague of McGavran's at Fuller Theological Seminary. Tippett points out that India still conditions McGavran's thought and behavior. Hence, if we would understand McGavran, we shall have to realize that his emphasis upon church growth began on a Third World mission field in India. This accounts in some measure for church growth's earlier identification with *mass* movements, *people* movements, and *group* conversion.[9]

The Institute

McGavran became a professor at the College of Missions in Indianapolis in 1957. He had received his M.A.

degree from that institution in 1923, prior to his appointment to India. This professorship permitted McGavran to travel and teach missions at various schools, especially those of his own denomination. It was during this period that McGavran conceived the idea of founding the Institute of Church Growth.

Northwest Christian College in Eugene, Oregon, invited McGavran to locate his Institute of Church Growth on its campus. The founding year was 1960, but operations began in 1961.

In 1965 McGavran was invited to move his Institute of Church Growth to Fuller Theological Seminary in Pasadena, California and to become the founding dean of Fuller Seminary's School of World Mission. More than 400 foreign missionaries and nationals from over forty mission boards have spent a year or more studying at the seminary's School of World Mission under McGavran and his colleagues. By 1973 over a hundred case studies and degree theses in missiology had been produced under Professor McGavran and his colleagues at Fuller. More than sixty books had also been published by McGavran's students.[10]

The Bulletin

The bulletin to which I refer is the *Global Church Growth Bulletin*, which McGavran began in 1964. It is a bimonthly, sixteen-page publication edited by McGavran. The number of subscribers now ranges between 6,000 to 10,000. About half of the subscribers are Americans. It is McGavran's primary vehicle for the spread of church growth ideas.

One should not confuse McGavran's *Global Church Growth Bulletin* with *Church Growth: America*, a magazine edited by W. Charles Arn and published by the Institute for American Church Growth. All issues of the *Global Church Growth Bulletin* through July of 1975 have been compiled and published in two separate volumes by William Carey Library. These two volumes constitute the best continuing history of the church growth movement. A third volume containing the issues since 1975 has been announced.[11]

The School

The school is the School of World Mission at Fuller Theological Seminary in Pasadena, California. Fuller Seminary bears the name of Charles E. Fuller who originated *The Old Fashioned Revival Hour.* Fuller is one of the largest and most highly respected nondenominational seminaries in the world.

Nothing of greater importance has happened to McGavran's church growth emphasis than his move to the Fuller stronghold in Pasadena. Several significant organizations and services have evolved from the School of World Mission and clustered in or near Pasadena. These are: William Carey Library, founded in 1969 by Ralph D. Winter, and the foremost publisher of church growth literature in the the world; the Church Growth Book Club, founded in 1970, and the least expensive outlet for books on church growth; the Institute for American Church Growth, founded by Win Arn in 1973; the American Church Growth Book Club, a 1973 subsidiary of the Church Growth Book Club; a Department of Church Growth in the Fuller Evangelistic Association which was added in 1976; the Missions Advanced Research and Communications Center (MARC), a ministry of the Evangelism and Research Division of World Vision International; and the U. S. Center for World Mission, founded by Ralph D. Winter.[12]

Perhaps in this context we should also mention that TEE (Theological Education Through Extension) has received much impetus from the church growth scholars at Fuller. TEE has grown rapidly on the foreign mission fields.

All of these auxiliary church growth ministries have naturally clustered around Fuller Seminary in Pasadena. While they are autonomous legal entities, most of them are interlocked through their staff personnel or through their boards. By far, the most vigorous and influential of these auxiliaries is the Institute for American Church Growth, headed by Win Arn.

The Book

The book is McGavran's *Understanding Church Growth*, published by Wm. B. Eerdmans Publishing Company in 1970.[13] *Understanding Church Growth* is the definitive work which sets forth the mature thought of McGavran on church growth. An editorial in *Eternity* magazine says this book gives the methodological hows, the sociological whys, and the theological oughts of church growth.[14] Peter Wagner says:"It must be considered the Magna Carta of the church growth movement."[15]

Summary

The fountainhead of the church growth river is Donald A. McGavran, the father of the church growth movement. Headwaters of the church growth river are closely tied to McGavran, the Institute of Church Growth, the *Global Church Growth Bulletin*, Fuller Seminary's School of World Mission, and the book *Understanding Church Growth*.

Church growth is a term created by McGavran to describe what he means by missions and evangelism. McGavran did not self-consciously set out to create a new movement or a new science. However, Pickett's research into mass movements in India so refreshed McGavran that what was then but a small stream for church growth has now become a large river.

2. Its Other Tributaries

The headwaters of the church growth river may be identified with a man, an institute, a bulletin, a school, and a book. Nevertheless, there are other streams and tributaries which feed the river. The four major ones which I shall treat are a new kind of evangelical ecumenicity, the superchurches, lay-witness training, and lay renewal; the three minor ones are neo-Pentecostalism, the Sunday School, and the Keswick Movement.

Evangelical Ecumenicity

A new kind of evangelical ecumenism is a little-known tributary feeding into the church growth river. Billy Graham incarnates an ecumenism which is quite different than that represented by the World Council of Churches and the National Council of Churches. Nor is Mr. Graham's ecumenism to be equated with that of the National Association of Evangelicals. Rather, it is more like that ecumenism which D. L. Moody set into motion, and which resulted in the founding of the International Missionary Council at Edinburgh in 1910.

Indeed, Mr. Graham and his organization were the architects for the Berlin Congress on World Evangelism in 1966 and the International Congress on World Evangelization at Lausanne in 1974. Five significant things for church growth happened as a result of those two meetings.

First, out of those meetings have come the various national congresses on evangelism such as those held in Amsterdam, Durban, Minneapolis, Ottawa, Lagos,

Manila, Singapore, Bangkok, Bogota, St. Andrews, Sydney, and so forth. Second, the two congresses brought evangelical Christian leaders together—many of them for the first time. They got to know and began to trust each other.

Third, a Lausanne Covenant was drawn up to spell out the theological commitment of the representatives and to invite others to make a similar commitment. Fourth, some church growth scholars such as Donald A. Mc-Gavran, Ralph Winter, and Orlando Costas were given an international platform for sharing their ideas at Lausanne.

Fifth, and potentially of great importance to church growth, a continuing Lausanne Committee for World Evangelization was established with Leighton Ford as chairman and Gottfried Osei-Mensah as executive secretary. Regular meetings of the committee are held. A variety of denominations and parachurch groups are represented on the committee.

Occasional papers are published by the committee. It was no accident that the first of those papers is titled *The Pasadena Consultation—Homogeneous Unit,* and the second titled *The Willowbank Report—Gospel and Culture.*[1] These papers deal forthrightly with some of the stickiest and most controversial elements in the church growth river.

Future congresses on evangelism, both worldwide and area-wide or national, may be planned by the Lausanne Committee. It becomes increasingly evident that what we may have in this committee is a prototype evangelical rival to the World Council of Churches. Hence, in the last two decades which have seen the gradual fall of the old ecumenical movement, a new phoenix has begun to rise above the planet—a creature which may be called the new evangelical ecumenism.

One should not think that the new ecumenism, gathered as it is around the powerful magnet of evangelism, is just "out there" somewhere. It is probably more "in here" than any ecumenism experienced hitherto by many of us.

Since Jimmy Carter became President, almost the whole world knows that Southern Baptists have always kept a safe distance from councils of churches. However, it might surprise some to know that Southern Baptist evangelism leaders were well represented at both Berlin and Lausanne. Nor did most of these leaders participate at their own expense. This time we are on the inside, and not solely because Billy Graham happens to be one of us. The climate has changed, and Southern Baptists are changing.

Key 73 is an example in embryo of the new evangelical ecumenism. Carl F. H. Henry, early in the decade from his post as editor of *Christianity Today,* pled with Evangelicals to somehow get together. They did get together for Key 73, an evangelistic effort by certain Evangelicals throughout America. The result was what Peter Wagner calls the disease of "hyper-cooperativism."[2] Even Southern Baptists and Missouri Synod Lutherans joined in Key 73. Parachurch groups such as Campus Crusade worked along with United Methodists and the Lutheran Church in America.

One very positive thing came out of Key 73. Some national and state denominational leaders got to know and trust each other under the umbrella of evangelism. The kind of grass-roots ecumenicity represented in a local Billy Graham crusade was now projected to the state and the nation. A reservoir of goodwill was built, from which we are still drinking.

My guess is that Key 73 helped pave the way for "Here's Life America." This large charismatic meeting held in Kansas City's Arrowhead Stadium during the summer of 1977 was an expression of the new evangelical ecumenism of America. About 45,000 classical Pentecostals and neo-Pentecostals gathered in Kansas City to celebrate their faith and to fellowship together. Most of them were Catholics. Many were members of mainline Protestant churches. Some were members of the traditional Pentecostal type denominations. These charismatics represent the right wing of America's new evangelical ecumenism.

The older ecumenism with its councils of churches does appear to be on the way out. The Consultation on Church Union (COCU), involving the merger of possibly ten denominations, never got off the ground. The best Jean Caffey Lyles can say about COCU is that it is moving "with all due reverent speed."[3] Organizations have been formed and financed in almost every major Protestant denomination to protest "theological liberalism." This breakdown of the "old" has contributed to the resurrection of the "new." Furthermore, the "new" is contributing to the swelling of the church growth river.

Superchurches

Superchurches are a second tributary feeding the church growth river. Some examples are Robert Schuller's Garden Grove Community Church in Orange County, California; Jack Hyles' First Baptist Church, Hammond, Indiana; Jerry Falwell's Thomas Road Baptist Church, Lynchburg, Virginia; Rex Humbard's Cathedral of Tomorrow, Akron, Ohio; Lee Roberson's Temple Baptist Church, Chattanooga, Tennessee; Harold Fickett's (and now Jess Moody's) First Baptist Church, Van Nuys, California; W. A. Criswell's First Baptist Church, Dallas, Texas; and James Kennedy's Coral Ridge Presbyterian Church, Fort Lauderdale, Florida.

Elmer Towns, an outspoken advocate of the superchurches, calls them "super-aggressive churches."[4] That they are superaggressive in their outreach can hardly be denied. When Towns wrote his study of the ten largest Sunday Schools in 1969, he said: "Six of the Sunday Schools among the ten largest are listed in the yearbook of the Baptist Bible Fellowship, Springfield, Missouri. Only one of the ten largest Sunday Schools is from a Southern Baptist Church."[5] Nine of the ten were Baptist, and five of the ten listed are from the eight examples given in the preceding paragraph.

Several common features may be noted about such superchurches. They have a strong and highly visible pastor. Their pastors stay put and don't move like rolling stones. Their present pastor may even be their founding shepherd.

While such churches may be aligned with a denomination, they tend to function as a minidenomination. They have large staffs and minister to everyone from the cradle to the grave. Often they own and operate schools such as kindergartens, grade schools, colleges, and even seminaries.[6] Most of them are vigorous in their use of mass media such as television and radio. Some of them own and operate their own printing presses. They might even have satellite churches and chapels under their tutelage. If they do belong to a denomination, their denomination needs them more than they need it.[7]

These superchurches are a potent force in church growth. Most of them conduct their own "how to do it" training events which attract hundreds and even thousands of participants annually.

They are living models of church growth. Many pastors and lay leaders of smaller and newer churches seek to pattern after them. Particularly is this modeling seen among the younger pastors and in those churches which do not exhibit a fierce denominational loyalty.

Take the method of bus ministry for example. Some of the superchurches have pioneered in using buses to achieve church growth. Temple, Thomas Road, and First

Baptist, Hammond are very strong on bus evangelism. Falwell's church has 125 old, reconditioned buses. During the late 1960s and the early 1970s, literally hundreds of churches sought to grow by instituting bus ministries modeled after these superchurches.

Perhaps at this point a word of caution should be spoken. Calvin Miller examines seven various models for church growth. Four of Miller's models are from the eight examples listed. Miller concludes that: "The best strategy for church growth does not lie in xeroxing other programs, but in observing the methods of those churches that are growing and applying their best principles to a situation."[8]

Lay-Witness Training

Lay-witness training is a third tributary to the church growth river. While lay-witness training goes all the way back to Jesus sending out the seventy (Luke 10:1-24), it took several giant strides forward in the seventies. It is now thoroughly institutionalized through such organizations as Evangelism Explosion III, International, the Billy Graham Evangelistic Association, Campus Crusade for Christ, and denominational programs such as the Southern Baptists' WIN (Witness Involvement Now) and TELL (Training Evangelistic Lay Leadership).

Four elements which stand out in today's lay-witness training are on-the-job training, an emphasis upon spiritual multiplication, the sharing of the gospel through the use of one's testimony and a booklet, and the use of transferable concepts. A missing element in so much of the lay-witness training prior to the seventies was learning how to witness through actual on-the-job training. Nowadays, the recognized ideal is to have a trained witness model for the trainee, showing how to do it in a living encounter with an unbeliever.

Spiritual multiplication has at least four aspects. First,

it is assumed in most lay-witness training such as EE and WIN that it is more important to train someone to lead another to Christ than it is to lead one to Christ. Second, trained witnesses are encouraged to always take a trainee with them. The Kennedy approach is to visit in threes because a trainer can teach two trainees in about the same time as he or she can train one. Thus, ultimately, spiritual mulitplication is achieved faster. Third, immediate and long-term follow-up are built into the training. Fourth, much material and more than one dozen models for follow-up are now available. Dawson Trotman and the Navigators deserve more credit for recovering this emphasis upon spiritual multiplication than any other person or group. The idea is caught up in the golden text of the Navigators (2 Tim. 2:2).

Using one's testimony and a booklet such as "The Four Laws," "The Bridge to Life," "Steps to Peace with God," or "How to Have a Full and Meaningful Life," is characteristic of much lay-witness training today. The personal testimony is recognized as the most useful tool the Christian has in sharing his or her faith. The testimony is considered as my story which has intersected and interfaced with the gospel story. The booklet is an organized outline of Scripture references, presenting such items as a plan of salvation, a call to Christian commitment, a model prayer of confession, some assurances of salvation, some disciplines called for if the new Christian is to grow in grace, and sometimes a blank page on which may be written the new convert's spiritual birth certificate.

Transferable concepts is a fourth element which stands out in lay-witness training today. EE's five-point outline of the gospel message is a transferable concept. You can memorize that outline and then transfer it to another Christian who can, in turn, pass it on. Dr. Bright of Campus Crusade makes frequent use of transferable concepts in his leadership. I have personally used the transferable concept of FORM in lay-witness training for more than eight years in about eighty lay evangelism schools. FORM is an acrostic where the F stands for family, the O for occupation, the R for religion, and the M for message—the message of the gospel. FORM is the witnessing track on which I usually operate. The F and the O are small talk. The R and the M are big talk. My destination in a witnessing encounter is to share the message of the gospel. However, the witnessing train must usually first pass through the other three prior stops.

Many thousands of Christians now have at least one intentional technique for sharing their faith face to face. I have myself been privileged to lead in the training of several thousand during the past decade. I know that the training is more thorough, more lasting, and of a better quality than that which I did in the decades of the fifties and the sixties.

Anglican Bishop Maurice A. P. Wood reminds us that "like speaks to like" in lay training for evangelism.[9] Many local churches of almost every denomination in North America are getting serious about implementing that principle through lay-witness training.[10]

One of the most interesting findings of the 1938 Tambaram meeting of the International Missionary Council said: "We are of the opinion that every phase of evangelistic work should be shared by both *men and women,* and that there should be equal opportunity of service for both men and women in this as in every department of the churches' activities."[11] That report was even more specific in saying: "The most effective approach to women is by women," and "The family must be evangelized as a family . . . ."[12] Scores of churches are seeking to equip men, women, and older youth to intentionally share their faith. There is no question but that such lay-witness training is a fresh and sweet-water stream flowing into the larger river of church growth.

Lay Renewal

Lay renewal is a fourth tributary which feeds into the church growth river. This stream includes such groups as Faith at Work, Laity Lodge, the Yokefellows, the Institute for Church Renewal, and the various denominational renewal emphases.

The lay renewal movement has turned on many persons to Christ and given them a structured means to share their faith with other Christians through lay renewal weekends and lay-witness missions. Denominations such as Southern Baptists, United Methodists, and Episcopalians now have their own denominational approaches to lay renewal. Churches of these denominations no longer have to call upon parachurch organizations such as the Institute for Church Renewal to serve their lay renewal needs.

Lay Renewal Weekends were introduced to many churches during the decade of the seventies. Some preferred to call them Lay Witness Missions. The LRW's struck evangelistic fire in some churches. So much so, that in some instances they replaced the revival meeting and produced far greater fruit than a traditional revival. A team of witnesses is engaged to come from other churches at their own expense during a LRW. As many as a hundred men, women, and youth may come to a large church. They minister from Friday night through Sunday noon. The witnesses stay in the homes of the host church.

The whole lay renewal movement is finally getting pastors and other church leaders to see themselves as equippers of others for the work of ministry. More are now willing to drop the first comma in Ephesians 4:12. The impact of men such as Sam Shoemaker, Elton

Trueblood, Findley Edge, Howard Butt, and Keith Miller is now at long last being felt.

While the roots of lay renewal can be traced back organizationally to Frank Buchman's Oxford Group,[13] it is striking to note that the first full-scale Protestant theology of the laity was not published until 1958.[14] Yet, the breeze of God's Spirit has been blowing across his church.[15] There is now no paucity of literature on the subject. Indeed, we might say that some churches are experiencing a new springtime. The gentle rains of lay renewal are falling and refreshing the church. These waters are gathering into a tributary which flows directly into the church growth river.

Neo-Pentecostalism

Doubtlessly, there are other tributaries which feed the church growth river. Neo-Pentecostalism should not be ignored. Both neo-Pentecostalism and the church growth movement are religious phenomena which arose simultaneously in this second half of the twentieth century. The new Pentecostalism has made it possible for the old, classical Pentecostalism to significantly influence the mainline Protestant and Catholic churches. The renewed and widespread emphasis upon spiritual gifts, attention to what is now being called "body evangelism," and the mushrooming of conferences on the Holy Spirit and the "deeper life," reveal the pervasive influence of Pentecostalism upon church growth.

Even the charismatic movement, as institutionalized through such parachurch groups as the Full Gospel Business Men's Fellowship International, Women Aglow, PTL, and The 700 Club, must be credited with some influence toward church growth. Charismatic parachurch personalities such as the late Kathryn Kuhlman, Oral Roberts, Pat Robertson, and Jim Bakker have become national celebrities.

Sunday School

A case might be made for singling out the Sunday School movement as a major tributary toward the church growth river. Especially would this be the case with those denominations which have tenaciously insisted that the Sunday School ought to be an outreach and evangelistic agency of the church. The historical and traditional approach of the Southern Baptist Sunday School Board toward religious education institutionalizes and incarnates that insistence. Therefore, all Sunday Schools geared toward evangelism and missions are doing church growth, albeit under a different nomenclature.

Specifically, we should single out bus ministry and children's worship as church growth agents. Usually both of these function under or through the administration of the Sunday School. Both of them are so widespread that together they constitute a sizable tributary toward church growth. Perhaps we should say a bit more about each of these new tools.

The decade of the seventies began with bus evangelism in its embryo stage. Gas was plentiful and cheap. Old public school buses could be bought for several hundred dollars. The Independent Baptists and Bible Baptists began it on a large scale. Southern Baptists began to experiment with it. The Evangelism Division of the Southern Baptist Home Mission Board promoted it. D. Lewis White was assigned to work with it at the Baptist Sunday School Board in Nashville. By the time bus evangelism had peaked among Southern Baptists around the midseventies, perhaps up to 20 percent of the Southern Baptist churches in some state conventions had experimented with a bus ministry.

Other groups such as the Nazarenes, the Assemblies of God, the Freewill Baptists, and the Pentecostal denomination also began bus ministries. Few, if any, United Methodists, Presbyterians, Lutherans, Episcopalians, or Catholics tried it. Nevertheless, a literature, a methodology, and a new paid, church-related vocation arose out of bus evangelism.

Concomitant with the advent of bus evangelism sprang up children's worship services in the churches. Having children worship separated from the adults was a new thing under the sun. The larger churches graded their children by ages for their worship services. Thus, a new kind of children's crusade arose in conjunction with bus evangelism. Again, this new approach to children's worship meant new workers, new literature, and a new kind of evangelism geared to children.

Keswick Movement

The Keswick Movement, which arose in England during the 1870s, is another possible tributary.[16] Built around the motif of a spiritual clinic, participants in a Keswick convention are led through an extensive examination, are diagnosed, are handed the prescription, and are set on the road to health. There are some theological ties between the Keswick Movement and the modern charismatic movement.

Furthermore, there is a striking similarity between the Keswick Movement and the so-called "deeper life" conferences now being conducted in this country. Whatever they are called, whether "deeper life," "spiritual life," "Holy Spirit," or even "Keswick," they are modeled after Keswick of England.

I believe such conferences represent a different brand of church renewal than that espoused by Shoemaker and Trueblood. It is also a brand which may appeal to a larger number of Christians in this country. Some of its best-known practitioners among Southern Baptists are Miss Bertha Smith, Peter Lord, Cecil McGee, and Jack Taylor.

Although the Keswick approach, as is often the case with neo-Pentecostalism and the more standard brand of lay renewal, is primarily focused on internal growth, it has great potential for empowering Christians to turn outward in expansion, extension, and bridging growth.

3. A Major Turn in Its Course

The church growth river took a major turn during the years 1972 and 1973. That turn was toward North America. However, before we go further, let us recapitulate what has been said thus far.

I have indicated that the term "church growth" originated with Donald McGavran on the mission field in India. McGavran did not self-consciously seek to start a movement. He was trying to find a term which would convey the content and substance which the words *missions* and *evangelism* once had, before liberal churchmen began to redefine them. McGavran incarnated church growth in his own life and life-style. He institutionalized church growth in 1960 with the formation of his Institute of Church Growth at Northwest Christian College in Eugene, Oregon. He set the foundations and parameters for church growth in 1970 in his definitive book *Understanding Church Growth*. McGavran has promoted and propagandized church growth through his *Global Church Growth Bulletin* since its first issue in 1964. But, McGavran has done nothing so important to his term "church growth" as founding the School of World Mission at Fuller Theological Seminary and moving his Institute of Church Growth to Pasadena in 1965.

Additionally, I hope I have begun to show that while the term "church growth" originated with McGavran, church growth is not the exclusive property of McGavran and his colleagues. There are others who share ownership of the concept, and especially those conservative and evangelical Christians who are doing church growth under the headings of missions, evangelism, and religious education.

Now, let us examine that decisive turn in course and look more carefully at what happened in those pivotal years 1972-73. Prior to 1972, in fact as early as the late fifties, Dr. McGavran's students who were preparing for the ministry in America frequently said to him: "The principles you teach apply here."[1] McGavran, of course, knew that, but the time was not ripe. Peter Wagner says: "In 1963 he planned to add to the Institute of Church Growth at Eugene an American Division headed by an American minister of church growth convictions, but the plan did not mature."[2]

It was not until late 1972 that McGavran felt he could turn his attention to America, and that the church growth river really rounded a bend. During the fall of 1972, Peter Wagner and Donald McGavran team-taught "a pilot course in church growth designed specifically for American church leaders."[3] Among the students in that course were Win Arn and Phil Goble. Arn has become the foremost promoter of church growth in America. Goble has pioneered a new model for Jewish evangelism called "the Messianic synagogue."

Prior to 1972 McGavran and his colleagues had directed their research primarily to the foreign mission fields. There were no books or published articles applying church growth thought exclusively to this continent. Then, in 1972, Paul Benjamin's, *The Growing Congregation,* was published.[4] Benjamin was professor of New Testament and Church Growth at Lincoln Christian Seminary, Lincoln, Illinois. His book "is the first direct effort to apply church growth principles to the American context by a denominational publishing house."[5]

One way to grasp the significance of this 1972 change in course for the church growth river is to contrast the content and style of McGavran's first well-known 1955 book, *The Bridges of God*,[6] with his 1973 book, *How to Grow a Church,* jointly authored with Win Arn.[7]

McGavran in *The Bridges of God* argued that "People Movements" should replace the old, antiquated "Mission Station" approach to missions. *The Bridges of God* created a sensation among missiologists. Not since Roland Allen, had any missionary been so bold and outspoken. McGavran felt that the world would never be won to Christ by picking off disciples one by one. Rather, he argued that the natural web of kinship and friendship in families, tribes, clans, and castes is the bridge across which God moves into the lives of unbelievers. He saw persons coming to Christ through what has come to be called "multi-individual mutually interdependent decisions." In fact, McGavran said people movements "have provided over 90 percent of the growth of the newer churches through the world. The great bulk of the membership and of the congregations of the younger churches consists of converts and the descendants of converts won in People Movements."[8] That kind of thought doesn't sound too relevant to the United States of America, does it? Well, that's the way McGavran's church growth was until 1972.

When you set over against *The Bridges of God* the book *How to Grow a Church,* the contrast is startling. The later volume is done in a conversational tone as a dialogue between McGavran and Arn. It is clearly designed for lay consumption. Techical terms and new phrases are carefully explained—almost to the point of condescension. They are all applied to America. The publisher can truthfully say in his "Foreword": "Reproducible principles of growth which have proven successful across the world are *now* focused on the American scene through this book."[9]

Two other events mark the year of 1972. Paul Benjamin in 1972 formed his own organization, called the National

Church Growth Research Center, headquartered at first in Cincinnati, Ohio, then in Lincoln, Illinois, and moved to Washington, DC in 1974.[10] Benjamin and his organization are primarily concerned with church growth in America.

Another important publishing event of 1972 was Dean Kelley's *Why Conservative Churches Are Growing.*[11] Kelley's book created quite a sensation—partly because of who he is and partly because of what he said. Kelley is an executive employed by the National Council of Churches. His thesis is that the more conservative churches are growing today because of their strict requirements for membership.

Some of Kelley's fellow churchmen have criticized and condemned the book, whereas Evangelicals and even Fundamentalists have commended it and quoted it approvingly.

Aside from the publication of McGavran and Arn's *How to Grow a Church,* two other major events which made 1973 a watershed year for church growth in America were the founding of the influential Institute for American Church Growth and the publication of a manual by Vergil Gerber. Win Arn, a doctoral student of Professor McGavran at Fuller, founded the Institute for American Church Growth.[12] Arn's explicit purpose is to so package, popularize, and promote the growing research on church growth that the lay leaders of America's churches can digest and use it to fulfill the Great Commission here at home.

Gerber's 1973 manual was titled *A Manual for Evangelism/Church Growth.*[13] Apparently it was designed for use both here and abroad. Professor McGavran in his introduction says, "This manual will help ministers and missionaries at home and abroad lead Christians to focus on biblical goals and pierce through the fog of good intentions and rosy estimates to the actual situation."[14] Gerber was a Conservative Baptist foreign missionary to Latin America for twenty-five years. When he wrote the manual, he was serving simultaneously as executive director of Evangelical Missions Information Service and executive secretary of the Evangelical Committee on Latin America, both joint committees of the Interdenominational Foreign Mission Association and the Evangelical Foreign Missions Association.

Note that Gerber's manual antedates by three years the one by Smith entitled *A Manual for Church Growth Surveys,*[15] and by nearly five years the one by Chaney and Lewis entitled, *Manual for Design for Church Growth.*[16] Also, it is revealing that Gerber uses a slash to join the two terms.

To conclude, up until about seven years ago the church growth river was flowing primarily through the foreign mission fields overseas. The term was as familiar to missiologists as the term "General Motors" is to us. That may be the major reason so many of us are not intimately acquainted with the river. One of the things I am trying to suggest is that maybe you shouldn't feel too guilty if you don't know a great deal about church growth.

4. Where It Is Flowing Today (Part 1)

Where is the church growth river flowing today? Six answers may be given.

Foreign Mission Fields

First, the church growth river is still flowing swiftly on the foreign mission fields. Take the example of Plan Rosario in Argentina. Evangelist Luis Palau sought to wed traditional methods of mass evangelism with church growth concepts in Argentina. So far as we know that was the first such attempt to combine a mass crusade with the planting of new churches. Twenty-one new churches were planted in the experiment. A growth rate in excess of 14 percent was sustained by the churches during the year of Plan Rosario.[1]

Palau has continued to experiment with using mass evangelism to start new churches out of converts won. Professor McGavran reports approximately eighty churches planted in Uruguay.[2] New churches as deliberate goals of mass evangelism campaigns is something new. The whole church has a stake in that kind of experimentation.

The presses continue to roll out books and articles on church growth across the seas. Many of those who have studied at Fuller Seminary's School of World Mission have published books. A very large body of literature on church growth abroad has accumulated. William Carey Library continues to be the most prolific publisher of research on church growth by foreign missionaries. Three recent examples of this literature which may be cited are by Southern Baptist missionaries: *A Manual for Church Growth Surveys* by Ebbie C. Smith was published by William Carey Library in 1976. *Indonesian Revival: Why Two Million Came to Christ* by Avery T. Willis, Jr., was published by William Carey Library in 1977. *New Move Forward in Europe: Growth Patterns of German Speaking Baptists* in Europe by William L. Wagner was published by William Carey Library in 1978.[3]

Homogenization

A second answer is that the church growth river is rapidly becoming homogenized. There are no denominationally pure streams of church growth in the world. Everybody who wants to do church growth is drinking from everyone else's fountain.

For example, the Nazarenes, a Holiness denomination headquartered in Kansas City, have geared their entire denomination to church growth.[4] All of their district superintendents have been trained by Peter Wagner, and by Win Arn of the American Church Growth Institute. Win Arn comes out of the Evangelical Covenant Church. Beacon Hill Press, the Nazarene's denominational publishing house, came out in 1978 with a dynamic little study course book on church growth. It is entitled *Get Ready to Grow: Principles of Church Growth,* and is authored by Paul R. Orjala, professor of missions at the Nazarene Theological Seminary. In that volume you can see how the Nazarenes have homogenized church growth and created a model for church growth which fits their theology and unique needs.

A second example of this homogenization is Waldo J. Werning's *Vision and Strategy for Church Growth,* published by Moody Press in 1977. Werning is a Missouri Synod Lutheran executive. Although Werning's denominational publishing house did not publish his book, it is nevertheless an attempt by Werning to create an instrument for church growth among Missouri Synod Lutherans. If you read Werning, you can readily see that he is exceedingly eclectic, drawing from everywhere, including his own tradition.

Still a third example of homogenization in church growth is *The Pyramid Principle of Church Growth,* published by Bethany Fellowship, Incorporated in 1977. David A. Womack, who at the time the book was written was a high official in the Assembly of God denomination, is its author. Southern Baptists may see something of what they call the Flake Formula in that book. Womack doesn't mention Arthur Flake's five-point formula for Sunday School growth. Yet, it is clear that what he calls the pyramid principle involves finding the prospects, enlarging the organization, enlisting and training sufficient leaders, providing the space, and going after the prospects in visitation. Especially does Womack come down hard on balancing points two, three, and four with points one and five. While such homogenization may not be self-conscious, it is nevertheless evident.

Parachurch Organizations

A third answer is that church growth is becoming thoroughly institutionalized in several parachurch organizations. The most influential parachurch organization is by far the Institute for American Church Growth in Pasadena. A major new correspondence curriculum for training laity in church growth was unveiled in 1978. Ted Yamamori now heads up that institute's Center for American Church Growth Studies. Win Arn reports that more than 10,000 clergy and 50,000 lay leaders have been involved in training through pastors' conferences and church growth seminars. More than a million people have seen one or more of the films on church growth. One hundred thousand copies of the book, *How to Grow a Church,* have been printed. Two hundred fifty thousand copies of *Church Growth: America* magazine have been distributed. Ministries of the institute have extended to more than fifty denominations. A Church Growth Media PAC to teach twelve weeks of church growth in adult Sunday School has been marketed for well over a year. That curriculum pack sold for $97.50 in 1979. The tuition for attending a three-day Advanced Church Growth Seminar for Professionals was $145 in 1979.[5]

A second influential parachurch organization involved in church growth is Evangelism Explosion III, International. While EE's primary thrust is lay-witness training, increasingly church growth materials and the church growth terminology may be seen in *EE Update,* the organization's monthly newsletter. EE is now at work in fifty countries on five continents.

A third parachurch organization which was mentioned in Chapter 3 is Paul Benjamin's National Church Growth Research Center in Washington, D. C.[6] We also need to know that there is a fourth such organization called the Canadian Church Growth Center in Regina, Saskatchewan, founded by Dennis Oliver, a recipient of one of the first Doctor of Missiology degrees from Fuller Seminary's School of World Mission. Oliver publishes *Church Growth Canada,* a counterpart to McGavran's *Global Church Growth Bulletin.*[7]

Books and Articles

A fourth answer is that the church growth river is producing a spate of books and articles. When Professor McGavran spoke to the Academy for Evangelism in Theological Education in 1978, he said he had recently counted twenty-five books on American church growth. He also indicated that he had been interviewed by editors of three religious journals within the past twelve months.[8]

The Christian Ministry magazine devoted its first issue

of 1979 to a series of four substantive articles on church growth.[9] A magazine which first appeared in March 1979, was filled with material on church growth and promised a continuing series of articles on the subject.[10] The potentially important research on mainline Protestant church growth, done by the Hartford Seminary Foundation, was reported in a June 1979, issue of *The Christian Century*.[11] These are only representative of the articles appearing during the first half of 1979.

Almost anyone who has a manuscript on church growth can find a publisher today. One of my students asked me why Harper and Row would publish McGavran and Arn's *Ten Steps for Church Growth*.[12] Why not? It is one of the hottest items on the religious market.

It should be noted that even some of the denominationally owned publishing houses are now issuing books on church growth which enter into dialogue with McGavran and company. Broadman Press, owned by The Sunday School Board of the Southern Baptist Convention in Nashville, Tennessee, is a case in point. Between 1971 and 1978 Broadman released at least seven titles which clearly relate to church growth.[13] Four of the seven authors of those volumes enter into serious dialogue with other church growth literature.[14]

Seminary Curriculum

A fifth answer is that an ever-increasing number of seminaries and Bible schools are offering courses and seminars on church growth. Fuller is still the stronghold for studying church growth, but it is no longer the only place.[15]

Lincoln Christian College and Seminary and Milligan College, affiliated with McGavran's denomination, have been offering church growth training for a number of years. Such training is now being offered by Bethel Seminary in St. Paul and by the Nazarene Theological Seminary in Kansas City.

Seminars have been offered for many years at Winona Lake, Biola College, and the Alliance School of Missions at Nyack, New York. Wheaton College Graduate School has offered a credit seminar since 1972.

Columbia Bible College in Columbia, South Carolina, has begun to offer a course in the last four years. One summer it was taught by Dr. McGavran. President J. Robertson McQuilken, of that institution, wrote one of the earliest evaluations of church growth entitled, *Measuring the Church Growth Movement,* published by Moody Press in 1973.[16]

A course on church growth is taught by the Religious Education Departments at Golden Gate Baptist Theological Seminary and New Orleans Baptist Theological Seminary. Golden Gate also sponsors annually a Church Growth Dynamics Institute under the leadership of Bill Schweer, professor of evangelism. A continuing education event on church growth was held at The Southern Baptist Theological Seminary in Louisville in 1978. Professors Bryant Hicks and Lewis A. Drummond both worked with that meeting. Again in a 1980 continuing education event, Southern offered a series of lectures on "The Association and Church Growth" by Professor Russell Bennett. Also, an "Advanced Church Growth Seminar" was offered by Southern in the spring of 1980.

Professor R. Calvin Guy of Southwestern Baptist Theological Seminary has been a friend to church growth from its inception. I have heard Professor McGavran publicly give credit to Guy for keeping him from quitting when he was so discouraged.[17] Church growth has been taught at Southwestern through the regular courses in missions and evangelism. Southwestern established a World Missions/Church Growth Center in 1980 with Professor Guy as the founding director.

A two-day conference on "Church Growth Emphasis" was held at Southeastern Baptist Theological Seminary in the spring of 1979. Midwestern Baptist Theological

Seminary offered one elective course on church growth three times during 1978-1979. A three-day church growth seminar, which enrolled approximately 300 participants, was held at Midwestern in the spring of 1980.

Many missions, evangelism, and religious education professors are aware of the church growth phenomenon. The significant fact about church growth moving into the seminary curricula is the potential for guiding the movement and shoring up its biblical and theological foundations.

Denominational Agendas

A sixth answer is that the church growth river is getting on the agenda, and in a few cases moving toward the top of that agenda, in several denominations. The Nazarenes have been referred to above. This fast growing Holiness denomination now numbers about 600,000 worldwide. By the end of 1988 they aim to have 850,000 members and 6,500 churches in the United States, Canada, and Great Britain. The Nazarene Theological Seminary hosted Peter Wagner for a series of lectures on church growth in 1979. Instead of bootlegging church growth, the Nazarenes are mainlining it.

The Reformed Church in America presents an interesting approach to church growth. That denomination grew out of the Dutch Reformed Church in America. It is over 350 years old. It is the denomination out of which Theodore J. Frelinghuysen, of the first Great Awakening, ministered. It is the denominational home of Norman Vincent Peale and Robert H. Schuller. This 215,000 member denomination has raised six million dollars in a five-year church growth drive. It plans to start a minimum of twenty-five new churches a year. A Dallas project to start three new churches in Dallas, Texas, over a three-year period has a budget of $800,000. The three congregations have already begun.[18]

The United Methodist Church is debating church growth. George Hunter, formerly professor of evangelism at Perkins School of Theology and now the chief executive for evangelism for United Methodists, spoke on church growth to the council of bishops in 1977. Hunter's message sparked quite a debate.[19] Hunter spent a sabbatical studying with McGavran at Fuller. Abingdon Press published *The Contagious Congregation* by Hunter in 1979. He firmly intends to reverse the declining growth of United Methodists. United Methodists have lost one million members over the last decade.

The United Presbyterian Church, U.S.A. (UPUSA), lost one-half million members during the past ten years. Their 1975 General Assembly established a working committee on Church Growth. A preliminary recommendation from that committee was that their denominational seminaries offer courses on church growth. Their San Francisco Theological Seminary in San Anselmo has established a chair and employed a professor who will teach church growth, missions, and evangelism. The dean at San Anselmo is Browne Barr. Perhaps you read Professor Barr's controversial article in a 1977 issue of *The Christian Century,* entitled "Finding the Good at Garden Grove."[20] Robert Schuller was a prominent lecturer at San Anselmo when Barr was installed as dean. William Carey Library published in 1977 *The Church Growth Crisis in the American Church: A Presbyterian Case Study* by Foster H. Shannon, a UPUSA pastor in the San Jose area. It may be of some interest that at one time there were more UPUSA students at Fuller Seminary than from any other denomination.

The Assembly of God denomination has been represented in church growth literature by such spokesmen as David Womack and Melvin Hodges. During the fall of 1978, the Assemblies of God held a five-day conference in Kansas City on church growth. John Wimber, at that time head of the Fuller Evangelistic Association's Department of Church Growth, and Professor Peter Wagner of Fuller Seminary were the leaders for that meeting. It has been reported that the Assemblies of God are establishing an average of one new church per day in the world. That isn't bad for a denomination which can only trace its history back to the Azusa Street Revival, which broke out in 1906.

The Baptist General Conference should also be mentioned. These are the Baptists which up until 1940 called themselves Swedish Baptists. They were predominantly of Swedish descent. They almost stopped growing between 1920 and 1940. Around 1940 they began to turn over a new leaf. Missionaries were sent out. They started planting churches in America. During the last thirty years they have doubled. Right now the Baptist General Conference is in the midst of an aggressive denomination-wide church growth emphasis, labeled "Double in a Decade." They are planting churches in areas outside of their traditional territory. Two of their churches, for example, have been planted in St. Louis and three in the Kansas City area.[21]

The Christian and Missionary Alliance has an ambitious goal to double its adult constituency by 1987. Presently, they are ahead of schedule on that goal. The CMA's inclusive membership in North America jumped a record 7.9 percent during the 1979-80 year. This relatively small denomination (216,000 in North America) logged a 13.7 percent membership jump in its overseas churches during 1978. Church growth is very much on the CMA agenda.[22]

Even the Reorganized Church of Jesus Christ of Latter Day Saints has set an agenda around church growth throughout the 1980s. The RLDS has adopted the theme, "Faith to Grow" for the decade of the eighties. That slogan refers both to growth in faith and growth in overall numbers. This 220,000 member denomination intends to step up missionary activity at home and abroad.[23]

Summary

I have suggested that the church growth river is now flowing swiftly on the foreign mission fields; it is rapidly becoming homogenized; it is becoming firmly institutionalized in several parachurch groups; it is producing a spate of books and articles; it is moving into the curricula of Bible schools and seminaries; and it is finding its way onto the agenda of numerous denominations.

The way the church growth river is flowing onto the agenda of Southern Baptists was intentionally omitted in the foregoing discussion. That will be the subject of the next chapter.

5. Where It Is Flowing Today (Part 2)

Southern Baptists have always been heavily involved in church growth, albeit we have done church growth under the headings of missions, evangelism, and religious education. Particularly have we done church growth under such terms as church extension (missions), soul-winning (evangelism), and Sunday School (religious education).

Historical Excursus

The Sandy Creek Baptist Church of Sandy Creek, North Carolina, illustrates the concern of our forebears for church growth. Founded in 1755, Sandy Creek was the mother, grandmother, and great-grandmother of forty-two churches in seventeen years. One hundred and twenty-five ministers came from these churches![1] Surely that is the kind of explosive multiplication which fits what McGavran calls expansion and extension growth, and almost certainly what he calls internal and bridging growth.

Sandy Creek's phenomenal growth was achieved through what Southern Baptists today call missions and evangelism or, more specifically, church extension and soul-winning. These Separate Baptists, led by Shubal Stearns, were also revivalistically oriented.

These two emphases of missions and evangelism were later institutionalized in the Home Mission Board and the Foreign Mission Board of the Southern Baptist Convention. They were, and are, incarnated in the lives of many thousands of Southern Baptists. "Church growth has occurred among Baptists," as James E. Carter says, "because they have consciously concentrated on it. Southern Baptists have made missions and evangelism an article of faith along with belief in God, the Scriptures, and the church."[2]

Subsequently, as the denomination organized itself and grew, Southern Baptists created a new thing. That old saying that "There is nothing new under the sun" was proven to be untrue. William Preston Clemmons has shown that Southern Baptist Sunday School leaders from 1896-1926 guided Southern Baptists "to develop a type of Sunday school work that was significantly different from anything else in the world."[3]

Even during the years 1845-1896, when the emphases and purposes of our Sunday Schools were about the same as those of others in American Protestantism, Southern Baptists demonstrated a marked preference for an evangelistic emphasis due to the Separate Baptist tradition. Moreover, during the first quarter of the twentieth century, the Sunday School came to function as the soul-winning enlistment agency of the local Southern Baptist church. No longer was the Sunday School just the teaching agency. No longer was it primarily a children's affair.[4]

The Sunday School became the reaching out agency of the church. It was thoroughly integrated into the church. The pastor became its chief officer and teacher. It began to become a channel for the church and the denomination. As Clemmons says: "This understanding of the Sunday school as the 'inquirers class' of the church for reaching unenlisted adult Baptist church members and unsaved persons changed the work of the Sunday school from one of being the school of the church, to that of serving the agency for numerical growth and evangelism for the church and the denomination."[5]

Arthur Flake wrote his *Building a Standard Sunday School* in 1919. This is the same Flake who created what we have come to call the Flake Formula. "The main business of the Sunday School is to win the lost to Christ," said Flake. "That is what churches are for. It was Christ's one supreme mission," continued Flake.[6]

Hence, we can begin to see how that original Baptist passion for missions and evangelism becomes merged with the Sunday School. More importantly, the Sunday School becomes the great organizational channel for Southern Baptist missions and evangelism. Clemmons concludes that "by 1926, Southern Baptists had devised a Sunday school strategy that emphasized evangelism, numerical growth, and outreach. This was a strategy which they not only have retained even into the 1970's, but which has differed significantly from the Sunday School strategy in use by other Protestant denominations."[7]

Carter is surely correct when he points out that one distinctive between the church growth movement and Southern Baptists is "the approach of growing churches through the educational organizations of the local church."[8] The March-April 1980, special issue of *Church Growth: America*, strikingly illustrates this difference. That entire issue is devoted to "The Sunday School and Church Growth." Editor W. Charles Arn introduces the topic by saying: "This is a special and, I believe very important issue. . . . It is breaking ground in an entirely new area of church growth. As you will see . . . , one of the most neglected areas of applied growth thinking in the local church has been in the Sunday School. And time is running out. In the last 10 years Sunday School enrollment has declined by almost one-fourth. You can do that once, but you can't do it three more times."[9]

Arn's statement about "breaking ground in an entirely new area of church growth" also reveals that the church growth movement is just now coming to an area of church growth which Southern Baptists have magnified since the early 1900s. It is precisely at this point of Sunday School growth that Southern Baptists may now make their most worthy contribution to the whole church.[10]

Present Involvement

Now, having made that important historical excursus into Southern Baptist church growth, let me move on to indicate how Southern Baptists are presently involving persons from the American Church Growth Movement in their programs. Paul Benjamin in 1974 addressed Southern Baptist evangelism leaders on church growth in Washington, D.C. In 1975 Peter Wagner was a major speaker at the annual meeting of SBC evangelism leaders in Florida.

Florida Baptists began a special emphasis on church growth in 1977. John Wimber, a Quaker, was used to help launch that emphasis. Probably Florida is farther along in programming for church growth than any of the older SBC state conventions. Their leaders have exhibited creativity and courage in channeling religious education and evangelism toward church growth.

The North Central Thrust for seven Southern Baptist states was launched with an emphasis on church growth. Donald McGavran was a guest lecturer for the launching meeting.

The Kansas-Nebraska Southern Baptist Convention used Win Arn and others to assist them in developing a convention strategy for church growth in 1977 and 1978. Twelve state staff members, directors of missions, and other leaders from Kansas-Nebraska attended the Advanced Church Growth Seminar for Professionals in Pasadena, California, in January of 1978. Several top leaders of that convention have worked on their D.Min. degrees at Fuller in church growth.

Win Arn spoke to the Texas Baptist evangelism conference in 1978. Win Arn and the staff of the American Church Growth Institute are being used to conduct church growth seminars among Texas Baptists.

In addition, several Southern Baptist state conventions and agencies are aggressively developing and promoting major growth programs of their own.

Baptists in Louisiana have for several years uniquely combined Sunday School work and evangelism to achieve church growth. The North Carolina Baptist Convention adopted several church growth goals in 1977, looking toward the year 1982. Those recommendations were presented by an official, high-level Church Growth Commission. The Missouri Convention has begun to conduct an annual workshop on church growth through the Sunday School.

An ever-increasing number of staff members from the Home Mission Board, The Sunday School Board of the Southern Baptist Convention, the Foreign Mission Board, and the Woman's Missionary Union are getting acquainted with the various aspects of church growth. The Sunday School Board now has a growth section in both its Sunday School and Church Training departments.[11] The Home Mission Board's Section on Evangelism has for several years offered four-day seminars on "Growing an Evangelistic Church."

Those who work in church extension and language missions at the Home Mission Board are very conversant with the leading church growth spokesmen, and with all of the available resources on church growth. A number of Southern Baptist foreign missionaries have studied at Fuller Seminary's School of World Mission.

Key leaders from the staffs of the Home Mission Board and the Sunday School Board have been meeting together to work out a unified approach to church growth for Southern Baptists. During December of 1979, the top executives of the Baptist Sunday School Board and the Home Mission Board issued a joint statement entitled, "Growing Southern Baptist Churches." That document defines church growth, lifts up some biblical principles of church growth, lists the characteristics of growing churches, and suggests seven actions toward growth.

Southern Baptists are also being impacted by church growth in ways other than those above. SBC researchers and scholars are having to take cognizance of it. Materials on church growth from non-Baptist sources are being used by our churches. These materials include books, films, posters, games, correspondence courses, and curriculum packages. Scores of Southern Baptists are participating in non-Baptist sponsored church growth seminars. Some non-Baptist church growth leaders and organizations are promoting SBC models, methods, and authors.

Implications for the Future

It seems to me that church growth has at least six implications for Southern Baptists. First, there is no way we can honestly ignore it. Southern Baptists have a natural affinity for church growth. Theologically we are in the same ball park with McGavran and his colleagues. Southern Baptists have long been committed to Great Commission missions, evangelism, and religious education. This commitment is being expressed in plans for six regional Church Growth Conferences to be conducted across the Southern Baptist Convention.[12] Also a three-day associational church growth workshop is being designed to be conducted by all 1,200 associations in the Southern Baptist Convention. Research, insights, and understandings of the church growth movement can be a valuable asset to this emphasis if denominational leaders will use them.

Second, the church growth movement is in some ways

analogous to the Sunday School movement, the foreign missions movement, the youth group movement, and the laymen's movement. Each of these movements began outside the churches and apart from the denominations as such. Nevertheless, each of them found its place in the churches and in the denominations. It is a matter of record that some of God's best gifts to the denominations and churches have come from concerned individuals or groups rather than from the denominational leadership.

Third, the church growth movement is pushing Southern Baptists further out of their parochialism and into the mainstream of evangelical ecumenism. Southern Baptists have much to offer to non-Southern Baptist Christians. Other Christians are eager to learn from us. It could well be that we shall make our greatest contribution to other Christians via the church growth movement.

Fourth, the movement may make it imperative that the Home Mission Board and the Sunday School Board work together more closely in planning and promoting church growth through evangelism, missions, and religious education. If there is any church growth in the Southern Baptist Convention, it will not likely happen apart from the work assigned to these two boards! However, the last thing the Southern Baptist Convention needs is two boards promoting two or more philosophies and tracks for church growth.[13]

Fifth, the church growth movement could provide an umbrella term for Southern Baptists which may bring several of our boards and agencies under its shade and sphere. Such terms as evangelism, missions, discipleship, outreach, and so forth are no longer umbrella terms. No one of them is big enough or bold enough or neutral enough to shade us from the heat of our own "recent bad past." Church growth a la Southern Baptist would make ample room for all to stand under the one umbrella.

Sixth, the very least which the church growth movement implies for Southern Baptists is the loss of neutrality regarding it. Southern Baptists are too visible and too strong to exhibit neutrality toward such a pervasive force as the church growth movement. The veritable avalanche of books, which the movement has produced and which are eagerly gobbled up by the Christian public, will not go away. The films on church growth are widely circulated. The materials and products on church growth continue to flow out to our churches. Pragmatically, as well as theologically, Southern Baptists are mature enough to publicly embrace every positive contribution of the movement and to offer some contributions of their own to it.[14]

6. Its Strange Vocabulary

Every river has a language of its own. The vocabulary of the church growth river may sound strange. Part of that strangeness may be accounted for by the newness of the river; part of it may be due to its human architects.

Whatever the reason for such an abundance of technical terms, they are a part of the cacophony of sounds uttered by the church growth river, and we can't, like Humpty Dumpty, make the words mean what we choose.

> "There's glory for you!" remarked Humpty Dumpty.
> "I don't know what you mean by 'glory,' " Alice said.
> "I mean there's a nice knockdown argument for you," he replied.
> "But glory doesn't mean a 'nice knockdown argument,' " Alice objected.
> "When *I* use a word," he retorted, "it means just what I choose it to mean, neither more nor less."[1]

The most comprehensive and concise glossary on church growth may be found in McGavran and Arn's *Ten Steps for Church Growth*.[2] Let us build our own list, drawing from that glossary and from other sources.

Church Growth. McGavran says: "By 'church growth' we mean *a process of spiritual reproduction* whereby new congregations are formed." McGavran continues: "In our use of the term, a Church grows when it *multiplies* its membership and its congregation and then with ever-increasing power takes into itself converts in a widening stream."[3] Hence, church growth is a process of spiritual reproduction which produces Christian converts and Christian churches. It is emphatically not an event. Nor does it deal with spiritual addition. Rather, it deals with spiritual reproduction and multiplication.

Church Growth Conscience. McGavran asserts: "Fantastic increase of churches is obviously the will of God."[4] A church growth conscience is the conviction that it is God's will for his church to grow. An illustration of how one who has such a conscience may express it is seen in the following words from Louis King of the Christian and Missionary Alliance: "The church was meant to be a missionary movement. Into its soul was breathed the Master's words, 'Go.' The true church is not geared to standing still, for its very equilibrium depends upon forward motion. It will wobble only when speed is slacked; it will topple over into the ecclesiastical scrap pile if it stops."[5]

Church Growth Eyes. Sometimes the term is used in conjunction with the phrase, "discerning the body." Professor McGavran uses the terms almost synonymously. Both phrases are examples of how church growth science appropriates the medical model to express itself. Church growth eyes are "a characteristic of Christians who have achieved an ability to see the possibilities for growth, and to apply appropriate strategies to gain maximum results for Christ and His Church."[6]

The Institute for American Church Growth has created a card game called "Church Growth Eyes." The game may be used in groups to learn how to see through church growth eyes.

Some persons are blind to possibilities for growth, while others have eyes like eagle Scouts. If you can see the potential for growth, you have church growth eyes. If you are blind to the possibilities, you need church growth eyes.

Three Ways to Increase Numerical Church Growth. These are biological growth, transfer growth, and conversion growth. Biological growth is the children and youth of existing members coming into the church. Transfer growth is members of one church who unite with another. Whereas, conversion growth is the conversion of persons who are outsiders to the family of God.

Church growth people contend that in the United States of America through biological growth alone a church should grow about 2.5 percent annually. Transfer growth is not real growth for the whole church. Calvin Miller calls it "ledger growth."[7] Only through conversion growth can a church really grow as God wills. McGavran's classic question on this is: "Suppose the only Christians in the world were the children of the twelve apostles?"[8]

Three Ways to Decrease Numerical Church Growth. These are death, transfer, and reversion. A church or denomination may lose members by physical death, transfer of membership to another church or denomination, and through the renouncement of the Christian faith by its members.

So there are basically three ways to enter and three ways to exit. This assumes that excommunication is a part of reversion, and that restoration may be accounted for under one of the three ways of increase.

Four Types of Church Growth. The McGavran school has settled upon four major types of church growth. These are internal, expansion, extension, and bridging. Internal growth is a growth in grace. Expansion growth is the growth of a congregation through evangelism (with emphasis on conversion growth). Extension growth is growth through planting daughter churches in the same homogeneous group and geographical area. Bridging growth is establishing churches across cultural and geographical barriers.

Another way to conceive these four types is to think of bridging growth as foreign missions, extension growth as home, state, and local missions, expansion growth as the growth of one local church, and internal growth as the growth of the individual Christian, and the inside growth and development of the local congregation. It is also possible to think of bridging growth as growth of the church in "Samaria and to the end of the earth," extension growth as growth of the church "in all Judea," and expansion growth as growth of the church "in Jerusalem." According to that scheme from Acts 1:8, internal growth would be the growth of the church inside the church in its Jerusalem.

Orlando Costas offers a different scheme. Costas contends that the "holistic expansion" of the church encompasses the four major areas of numerical, organic, conceptual, and incarnational growth. By numerical expansion is meant "the recruitment of persons for the kingdom of God" and "their incorporation into a local community" of Christians. Essentially Costas means by numerical growth what the McGavran school means by expansion growth.

By organic expansion Costas means "the internal development of a local community of faith, that is, the system of relationships among its members" McGavran's internal growth type would probably correspond closely to the organic type.

By conceptual growth Costas means "the degree of consciousness that a community of faith has with regard to its nature and mission to the world." Costas has in mind the church's image of herself and her world, the depth of her reflection on the meaning of her faith, her knowledge of Scripture, etc. This idea has no direct correspondence to the McGavran types. However, conceptual growth definitely relates to McGavran's bridging, extension, and expansion types.

By incarnational growth Costas means the church's involvement "in the life and problems of her social environment." Costas has in mind the church's prophetic function. His paradigm for incarnational growth is Luke 4:18-21. McGavran has no type which corresponds to this.[9]

Five Classes of Leaders. McGavran identifies five classes of church leaders. Class 1 is volunteer leaders headed inward. Class 2 is volunteer leaders headed outward. Class 3 may be partially paid leaders who work at secular occupations. Class 4 is full-time, paid church leaders. Class 5 is denominational or interdenominational leaders who work beyond one local church.

McGavran does not have in mind a hierarchy of church leaders. By classifying leaders thusly, he gives us an instrument to help us test the balance of our leadership between inreach and outreach functions in church growth.

Composite Membership. Membership figures alone do not tell much about a church. Charles Mylander in 1975 devised a more meaningful index called "composite membership." To find your composite membership, add your total church membership to your average worship attendance and to your average Sunday School attendance; then, divide by three.[10]

Take your total membership at the end of the year regardless of how you define members. Your average worship attendance for the year will include the summer slump and the Easter hump. Use your annual average Sunday School attendance, because that is more meaningful than your enrollment. Thus, if your church membership is 200, your average worship attendance 125, and your average Sunday School attendance 100, your composite membership is 142.

Decadal Growth Rate. The symbol for this is DGR. The decadal growth rate is the rate at which your church grew during the last decade. For example, suppose your membership is now 200, but ten years ago it was 100.

Your decadal growth was 100 percent. Take another example. Your membership is 500. Ten years ago it was 400. Your decadal growth rate was 25 percent.[11]

To calculate your DGR do these three steps: (1) Discover the difference between your membership now and ten years ago; (2) Divide that difference by the membership at the beginning of the decade; and, (3) Change the decimal to a percentage.[12]

Your DGR will give you a more accurate growth picture than just looking at one or two years, or even five years. It is what happens over the long pull that is of greater significance. The DGR will of course reveal decreases as well as increases.

Church Growth Rates. McGavran contends that biological growth alone should usually be calculated on the basis of 25 percent per decade. That would vary according to the population growth of the particular church. Nevertheless, it is a good place to begin. A DGR of 25 percent is barely growing at all.

Peter Wagner considers that a DGR of 50 percent in the United States is not too bad, "not really healthy . . . but not unhealthy." A DGR of 100 percent, Wagner thinks, is pretty good; 200 percent newsworthy; and 300 percent, "the pastor better prepare to hold seminars to share his methods with others."[13]

The Fourth World. The Fourth World is a term coined by Peter Wagner in 1972 to describe the world of lost persons—now perhaps at least 2.7 billion. Wagner points out that while Christianity is growing at the rate of 55,000 persons per day, the Fourth World is growing by 148,000 persons per day. Indeed, Bishop Chandu Ray says: "Ninety-eight percent of Asia is in the Fourth World."[14]

Wagner's term is useful in sensitizing our consciences to the plight of almost three fourths of the world's people. Besides the NATO, the Warsaw Pact, and the Third World nations (Asia, Africa, and Latin America), there is a

CHURCH GROWTH—A MIGHTY RIVER

Fourth World which so far as the light of the gospel of Christ goes is a world of utter darkness.

Homogeneous Unit. The symbol is HU in church growth jargon. McGavran defines an HU as a "section of society in which all the members have some characteristic in common." The HU, says McGavran, "may be a segment of society whose common characteristic is a culture or a language." It might be "a tribe or caste."[15]

Wagner defines an HU as "a group of people who consider each other to be 'our kind of people.' "[16] The HU gives rise to the homogeneous unit principle, which we shall discuss in chapter 9. Suffice it to say here that the HU is what permits McGavran to trumpet: "the Church should ride on the chariot of lineage and clan to a discipling of the tribes."[17]

Evangelism Zero, One, Two, Three. Symbols are E-0, E-1, E-2, and E-3. The church growth school now speaks of four classifications of evangelism. These classifications measure the cultural distance between the evangelist and the person or group being evangelized. E-0 is "winning nominal Christians back to fervent faith."[18]

E-1 is reaching out to one's "own kind of people." The evangelist "is talking to intimates, friends, business companions, uncles and aunts, sisters and cousins; to those who belong to his club or work in his factory or office. Here unstructured spontaneous evangelism functions well."

E-2 is evangelizing "other homogeneous units, other segments of society you seldom meet." They may speak English, but Spanish might be their mother tongue.

E-3 is evangelizing "where there are differences of language and race, as well as of wealth and education. It's the kind of evangelism one does when he goes to Africa, Singapore, or Japan."[19]

Occasionally the symbols M-0, M-1, M-2, and M-3 may be used to describe the same cultural distances in terms of missions. We shall have occasion to look more closely at the cultural element in evangelism in chapter 11.

Presence, Proclamation, and Persuasion Evangelism. A number of church growth leaders identify three basic methods of evangelism as presence, proclamation, and persuasion. Presence is considered a valid form in that it gives credibility to our witness. Taken by itself, however, presence does not usually produce disciples.

Proclamation is the verbalizing of the gospel. Its mildest form is dialogue. Orjala calls it "hit-and-run evangelism," and sees it as message-centered rather than person-centered.[20] Nevertheless, we do have a message to proclaim.

Persuasion is mentioned in the book of Acts as Paul's style. Paul says: "We persuade men" (2 Cor. 5:11). Probably the ideal would be for the church to aim for a balance of these three "Ps" in her evangelism.

Evangelism Potential. The symbol is EP. Most of us, it is assumed, are inside members of at least eight HUs (homogeneous units or areas of influence). Those HUs may be designated family/relatives, neighborhood, work/school, age, ethclass (i.e., ethnics + social class), origins, special interests, and trade/profession.

Look at each of these HUs and estimate how many persons in each HU you know who are not Christians. Orjala says the "average person's total of all groups is usually 100." The total is your personal evangelism potential. "Now calculate the EP of your church," says Orjala, "by multiplying the membership by 100. The total EP of your church is absolutely astounding."[21]

Removing the Fog. Fog is that which obscures reality in church growth. Fact gathering and fact analysis will remove the fog. This is where the manuals and survey forms come into the picture.[22] Those who have church growth eyes can discern both the body and the community, and therefore lift the fog.

CHURCH GROWTH—A MIGHTY RIVER

The Choke Law. A missionary in Tanzania "observed that as a church grows the existing members tend to absorb the entire time, attention, and budget of both laymen and pastors." Thus maintenance chokes off evangelism and growth ceases.[23] This is the choke law.

The choke law operates everywhere, on the foreign mission fields and here at home. Church leaders get involved with doing good things while the better and the best activities are choked out.

Body Evangelism. Wagner sees three streams of evangelism flowing through the past twenty-five years of church history. Crusade evangelism, identified with Billy Graham, appeared in the 1950s. Saturation evangelism, identified with Kenneth Strachan of the Latin American Mission, and expressed through emphases such as Evangelism in Depth and New Life for All, arose in the 1960s. Saturation evangelism came to America in Key 73. Then, body evangelism, which Wagner identifies with Vergil Gerber, appeared in the 1970s. "The major innovation of body evangelism" says Wagner, is that "it helps clarify the goal against which any method must be ruthlessly evaluated." That goal is church growth.[24]

Eurica and Africasia. McGavran likes to use the term Eurica as a single word for Europe and North America. The adjective Eurican is also used. Africasia means Africa, Latin America, and Asia.[25]

Ta Ethne. This is the Greek phrase in the Great Commission for the nations. McGavran frequently uses it as a technical phrase meaning the various ethnic groups such as families, castes, tribes, and the mosaic of different homogeneous units in society. The *ta ethne* are the non-Jews, the Gentiles. It is not a phrase, for example, synonymous with the more than 100 nations who belong to the United Nations.

The Bottom Line. In church growth the bottom line is the actual, factual growth of the church through new

Christians beginning a life-changing experience as responsible members of a local congregation. Church growth leaders are concerned with making disciples rather than counting decisions.

Receptivity. DuBose calls it "our view of 'God's open door.' "[26] The church growth point of view does not advocate abandonment of resistant fields. It does advocate holding them lightly. McGavran boldly asserts: "Gospel acceptors always have a higher priority than Gospel rejectors."[27]

The idea of receptivity gives rise to the principle of receptivity with which we shall deal in chapter 9.

Conclusion

There are other terms which have technical meanings. Such phrases as "people movements," "group conversion," "the power encounter," "discipling," "perfecting," "folding," "the bridges of God," and "multiindividual, mutually-interdependent decision," need some explanation. Also the whole "pathology of church growth" deserves attention. We shall have occasion to look at most of these phrases in the remaining chapters.

7. Its Biblical Basin

The church growth river flows in a biblical basin. Alan Tippett says the evidence for church growth from the Bible is declarative, implicative, precedential, or cumulative.

By *declarative evidence* Tippett means "a direct, specific, or categorical statement or an imperative." An example would be a form of the Great Commission such as: "Go therefore and make disciples of all nations" (Matt. 28:19).

By *implicative evidence* Tippett means "statements clearly implied in the passages cited." An example would be: "You are the light of the world" (Matt. 5:14). That statement implies that the Christian disciple has the role of driving away the darkness of the world, though it does not explicitly say so.

By *precedential evidence* Tippett means "God has shown his approval of, and set his Spirit on" certain methods recorded in Scripture. An example is the method of the Antioch missionary program. While the Antioch method may not be God's normative method, "the fact that he once blessed it indicates that it is in accord with his will at least for some situations."

By *cumulative evidence* Tippett means "the quantitative assembly of scriptural statements that point in a single direction and reinforce each other." An example is those passages which refer to the sacrifice of Christ for sin. Though such Scriptures may not use the word *love,* that "corpus of material demonstrates his great love for man."[1]

We shall examine some of that evidence in certain passages which may be labeled "grow in grace," "Great Commission," "great commandment," "numbering," "growth imagery," "diffusion," and "the children of promise." Each class of these passages will fit one or more of the types of church growth identified by Mc-Gavran and / or Costas.

Grow in Grace Passages

There are at least four texts which may be called grow in grace passages. These texts undergird what the McGavran school labels internal growth, and those aspects of "holistic expansion" which Costas labels organic and conceptual growth. The four references are 2 Peter 3:18*a;* 1 Peter 2:2; Ephesians 4:15-16; and 2 Thessalonians 1:3. Look at them:

1. 2 Peter 3:18*a.* "But grow in the grace and knowledge of our Lord and Savior Jesus Christ."
2. 1 Peter 2:2. "Like newborn babes, long for the pure spiritual milk, that by it you may grow up to salvation."
3. Ephesians 4:15-16. "We are to grow up in every way into him who is the head, into Christ . . . which . . . makes bodily growth and upbuilds itself in love."
4. 2 Thessalonians 1:3. "We are bound to give thanks to God always for you, brethren, as is fitting, because your faith is growing abundantly, and the love of every one of you for one another is increasing."

Great Commission Passages

Bridging, extension, and expansion growth are supported by the Great Commission passages. So are organic and conceptual growth. Traditionally, five forms of the Great Commission have been identified, one in each of the four Gospels and one in Acts. A sixth form of the commission may be singled out in Paul's letter to the Romans. The six passages are Matthew 28:18-20; Mark 16:15-18; Luke 24:46-49; John 20:21-23; Acts 1:8; and

Romans 15:18-21. Look at them:

1. Matthew 28:18-20. "And Jesus came and said to them, 'All authority in heaven and on earth has been given to me. Go therefore and make disciples of all nations, baptizing them in the name of the Father and of the Son and of the Holy Spirit, teaching them to observe all that I have commanded you; and lo, I am with you always, to the close of the age.' "
2. Mark 16:15-18. "Go into all the world and preach the gospel to the whole creation. He who believes and is baptized will be saved; but he who does not believe will be condemned. All these signs will accompany those who believe: in my name they will cast out demons; they will speak in new tongues; they will pick up serpents, and if they drink any deadly thing, it will not hurt them; they will lay their hands on the sick, and they will recover."
3. Luke 24:46-49. "Thus it is written, that the Christ should suffer and on the third day rise from the dead, and that repentance and forgiveness of sins should be preached in his name to all nations, beginning from Jerusalem. You are witnesses of these things. And behold, I send the promise of my Father upon you; but stay in the city, until you are clothed with power from on high."
4. John 20:21-23. "Jesus said to them again, 'Peace be with you. As the Father has sent me, even so I send you.' And when he had said this, he breathed on them, and said to them, 'Receive the Holy Spirit. If you forgive the sins of any, they are forgiven; if you retain the sins of any, they are retained.' "
5. Acts 1:8. "But you shall receive power when the Holy Spirit has come upon you; and you shall be my witnesses in Jerusalem and in all Judea and Samaria and to the end of the earth."
6. Romans 15:18-21. "For I will not venture to speak of anything except what Christ has wrought through me to win obedience from the Gentiles, by word and deed, by the power of signs and wonders, by the power of the Holy Spirit . . . as it is written, 'They shall see who have never been told of him, and they shall understand who have never heard of him.' "

McGavran reminds us that the phrase *ta ethne,* or "the

nations," in the Great Commission (according to Matthew) means the various ethnic groupings such as class, castes, tribes, etc. and is not necessarily the same as what we call nations today. That interpretation fits what McGavran says about the homogeneous unit, people movements, and group conversion.

Unfortunately, McGavran makes the mistake of dividing the Great Commission into two parts which he calls discipling and perfecting. The first part he says deals with discipling, and the second part with perfecting. The problem with that interpretation is that the phrases "baptizing them . . ." and "teaching them . . ." are not temporal, sequential phrases, but co-terminal phrases with the command "make disciples." Therefore, the text from Matthew actually says that baptizing into the name of the Trinity and teaching to observe the Commandments are two ways of making disciples.

Regarding the Markan text, it should be observed that some of the ancient manuscripts do not include the words. I include them so that they might be compared with the others.

When the six texts are taken together and examined for common features, the following outline emerges. The One who issues the Commission has the authority to give it. Elements of intentionality, universality, and supernatural power seem to characterize them. They are all given to the church, and the Commanding General who issues these orders expects them to be obeyed. Church growth, then, becomes a matter of obedience to the divine commission. Such interpretation leads to what is called Great Commission missions.

Great Commandment Passages

The same One who gave the Great Commission also gave the great commandment. This class of passages fits what Costas calls incarnational growth. While many texts may be cited, the two following are primary:

1. Matthew 22:37-40. "You shall love the Lord your God with all your heart, and with all your soul, and with all your mind. This is the great and first commandment. And a second is like it, You shall love your neighbor as yourself. On these two commandments depend all the law and the prophets."
2. 1 John 4:19-21. "We love, because he first loved us. If anyone says, 'I love God,' and hates his brother, he is a liar; for he who does not love his brother whom he has seen, cannot love God whom he has not seen. And this commandment we have from him, that he who loves God should love his brother also."

Deuteronomy 6:4-5 tells us to love God supremely. Leviticus 19:18 says: "You shall love your neighbor as yourself." Jesus combined the two. Moreover, Jesus tells us in Luke 10:29-37 who a neighbor is. A neighbor is the good Samaritan. James 2:8-9 refers to love for one's neighbor as "the royal law."

Luke 4:16-30 seems to indicate that Jesus conceived of his mission in terms of the twin love commandments. When John the Baptist doubted him, Jesus sent this proof to John: "Go and tell John what you hear and see: the blind receive their sight and the lame walk, lepers are cleansed and the deaf hear, and the dead are raised up, and the poor have good news preached to them. And blessed is he who takes no offense at me" (Matt. 11:4-6).

The judgment of the nations in Matthew 25:31-46 separates the goats and the sheep on this basis: "I was hungry and you gave me food, I was thirsty and you gave me drink, I was a stranger and you welcomed me, I was naked and you clothed me, I was sick and you visited me, I was in prison and you came to me" (vv. 36-37).

James 1:27 goes so far as to declare: "Religion that is pure and undefiled before God and the Father is like this: to visit orphans and widows in their affliction, and to keep oneself unstained from the world."

Dostoevski's Christ figure, Alyosha, was right. There is a difference between loving one close up and loving one at a distance, between loving one in his or her dreams and loving one in reality, between loving one with words and loving one with deeds. Church growth which does not exhibit this incarnational dimension is neither biblical nor Christian.

Numbering Passages

Expansion and numerical growth have strong scriptural support. Was Jesus successful by our numerical standards? You be the judge. Peter Wagner says: "Jesus began by winning 12 people to Himself. When he finished, the 12 had become a committed group in Jerusalem of no less than 120 disciples, but more probably upwards of 500—as hinted in I Corinthians 15:6. Growth from 12 to 120 in 3 years represents a decadal rate of 215,343% or an annual growth rate of 115%! This is astronomical enough without even figuring it on the basis of 500 instead of 120!"[2]

Let us choose from the many texts available in the book of Acts. I shall *italicize* some of the relevant phrases and add some comments as they might be appropriate.

1. 1:15. Of those in the upper room in Jerusalem it is written: "The company of persons was in all about a *hundred and twenty.*"
2. 2:41. Of those converts at Pentecost it is written: "So those who received his word were baptized, and there were added that day about *three thousand souls.*"
3. 2:47b. Following Pentecost it is written: "And the Lord added to their number *day by day* those who were being saved." Wagner says about 55,000 now become Christians every day.
4. 4:4. Following the healing of the man lame from birth, and upon the arrest of Peter and John near the Temple,

it is written: "But many of those who heard the word believed; and the number of the men came to about *five thousand.*" I take this to mean an *additional* 5,000 men, besides the women and children.

5. 5:14. Following the death of Ananias and Sapphira, it is written: "And more than ever believers were added to the Lord, *multitudes both of men and women.*"

6 6:1. The passage about the seven begins: "Now in these days when the disciples were increasing in number."

7. 6:7. Following the appointment of the seven, it is written: "And the word of God increased; and the number of the disciples *multiplied* greatly in Jerusalem, and a great many of the priests were obedient to the faith." Up to here disciples had been *added.* Now, they are *multiplied.* Josephus says there were 20,000 priests practicing at that time.

8. 9:31. Following Paul's visit to Jerusalem, it is written: "So *the church* throughout all Judea and Galilee and Samaria had peace and was built up; and walking in the fear of the Lord and in the comfort of the Holy Spirit *it* was multiplied." The church, meaning churches, is now multiplied, not just persons.

9. 9:35. Following the healing of Aeneas in Lydda, it is written: "And all the residents of Lydda and Sharon saw him, and they turned to the Lord." This may be an example of a people movement in the early church.

10. 16:5. Following the Jerusalem Conference, it is written: "So the churches were strengthened in the faith, and they increased in numbers daily."

11. 21:20*b*. To Paul it was said: "You see, brother, how many thousands there are among the Jews of those who have believed." The word for thousands here comes from the Greek word *myriads* which means tens of thousands.

We might also cite two other passages. In Luke 15 the sheep are counted exactly. That's the way the shepherd knew one was lost from the fold. First Peter 5:2 tells us to "tend the flock." One motive of numbering the sheep is pastoral care.

In the light of such passages as the above, is it any wonder that McGavran concludes: "Quantification does not depreciate spiritual qualities. Man is both a soul which cannot be measured and a body which can be"?[3] It is hard to see a problem until we quantify it. Even physicists quantify great ideas. Take, for example Einstein's theory of relativity—$E = mc^2$. Atomic energy could not be tapped until it was quantified.

Growth Imagery Passages

The Bible abounds with growth images in connection with the kingdom of God, and the church. While expansion growth is especially undergirded by such images, they lend support to all types of growth. Eugene Wright comments on growth images: "Analogies abound: seed, which first dies and then is transformed into new life and grows until harvest time; a mustard seed, which begins very small and becomes very large; yeast, which enlarges, permeates and grows in its penetrating power; Jesus as the vine and his disciples as the branches intended to bear fruit. The whole story of Pentecost, in which a few Christians became 3,000 and then 5,000, is the birth and paradigm of the church moving forward in the power of the Spirit."[4]

The following passages may be cited:

1. The church is called the body of Christ. For example, Paul in 1 Corinthians 12:27 says, "Now you are the body of Christ and individually members of it." Ephesians 4 speaks of "bodily growth" (v. 16). The purpose of spiritual gifts is "for building up the body of Christ" (v. 12). The goal of church growth is to attain "mature manhood," that is, "the measure of the stature of the fulness of Christ" (v. 13), who is the head of the church (v. 15).
2. The church is called a living temple by both Peter and Paul. Note what Peter says in 1 Peter 2:4-5: "Come to him, to that living stone, rejected by men but in God's sight chosen and precious; and like living stones be

yourselves built up into a spiritual house, to be a holy priesthood, to offer spiritual sacrifices acceptable to God through Jesus Christ.''

Paul's word in Ephesians 2:19-22 may be even stronger: ''So then you are no longer strangers and sojourners, but you are fellow citizens with the saints and members of the household of God, built upon the foundation of the apostles and prophets, Christ Jesus himself being the cornerstone, in whom the whole structure is joined together and grows into a holy temple in the Lord; in whom you also are built into it for a dwelling place of God in the Spirit.'' Not only are our bodies temples of the Holy Spirit, we are ourselves as the people of God a living, growing temple of the Holy Spirit.

3. Another outstanding growth imagery passage is 1 Corinthians 3:9, ''For we are God's fellow workers; you are God's field, God's building.'' We are God's acre, God's Taj Mahal.

Tom Houston examined some growth images in the parables of Jesus, such as the parables of the sower, the wheat and the weeds, the seed growing secretly, etc. He concluded that Jesus saw the kingdom of God as *always growing,* but that *not all growth is valuable.* Houston found three criteria by which nonacceptable growth may be identified: wealth, popularity, and activity and success.[5]

Diffusion Passages

These are texts which deal with spreading the knowledge of God's salvation to the ends of the earth. Especially prominent in such passages are the metaphors of light and darkness. They particularly undergird extension, bridging, and conceptual growth; but relate to all types of growth.

The following passages may be selected from a very large number of possibilities:

1. Isaiah 9:2. "The people who walked in darkness have seen a great light;
   those who dwelt in a land of deep darkness, / on them has light shined."
2. Matthew 4:13-16. "He [Jesus] went and dwelt in Capernaum by the sea, in the territory of Zebulun and Naphtali, that what was spoken by the prophet Isaiah might be fulfilled: 'The land of Zebulun and the land of Naphtali, / toward the sea, across the Jordan, / Galilee of the Gentiles—/ the people who sat in darkness / have seen a great light, / and for those who sat in the region and shadow of death / light has dawned.' "
3. Isaiah 42:6-7. "I am the Lord, I have called you in righteousness, / I have taken you by the hand and kept you; / I have given you as a covenant to the people, / a light to the nations, / to open the eyes that are blind, / to bring out the prisoners from the dungeon, / from the prison those who sit in darkness."
4. Isaiah 49:6b. "I will give you as a light to the nations, / that my salvation may reach to the end of the earth."
5. Acts 13:47-49. "For so the Lord has commanded us, saying, / 'I have set you to be a light for the Gentiles, / that you may bring salvation to the uttermost parts of the earth.' / And when the Gentiles heard this, they were glad and glorified the word of God; and as many as were ordained to eternal life believed. And the word of the Lord spread throughout all the region."
6. Acts 26:17-18. "Delivering you [Paul] from the people and from the Gentiles—to whom I send you to open their eyes, that they may turn from darkness to light and from the power of Satan to God, that they may receive forgiveness of sins and a place among those who are sanctified by faith in me."
7. John 8:12b. "I am the light of the world; he who follows me will not walk in darkness, but will have the light of life."
8. Matthew 5:14a. "You are the light of the world."
9. 1 Peter 2:9b. "That you may declare the wonderful deeds of him who called you out of darkness into his marvelous light."

Note the interplay of the two covenants in the above passages. The church is to pick up where the old Israel left off.

The Children of Promise Passages

A final class of passages which we shall lift up are those which refer to the children of promise. They are prophetic Scriptures which relate to God's covenant with his people.

Genesis 12:1-3 is God's covenant with Abram. God promised Abram: "I will make of you a great nation . . . and make your name great . . . by you all the families of the earth shall bless themselves" (vv. 2-3). That covenant is reaffirmed in Genesis 15:1-6. Abram was told: "Number the stars, if you are able to number them . . . so shall your descendants be" (v. 5).

The Abrahamic covenant was reconfirmed with Isaac in Genesis 26:1-5. The same promises were made to Isaac as to Abram. The same covenant was continued with Jacob in Genesis 28:10-17. Only instead of stars, Jacob was told: "your descendants shall be like the dust of the earth" (v. 14).

Paul, in Galatians 3:6-9 (and elsewhere), claimed these promises of the Abrahamic covenant for the Gentiles— the nations. He insisted that all men of faith are sons of Abraham, and that the gospel was preached beforehand to Abraham in that magnificent promise: "In you shall all the nations be blessed."

A most remarkable passage is Isaiah 54:1-3. C. H. Spurgeon preached a great sermon on 54:1, and William Carey used 54:2-3 as his text on May 31, 1792, when he preached on the theme: "Expect great things from God, and attempt great things for God." Paul, in Galatians 4:21-31 and Romans 9:6-13, applies 54:1 to the church, and says, "Now we, brethren, like Isaac, are children of promise."

Another great passage in this vein is Exodus 19:3-6. Peter, in 1 Peter 2:9-10, applies the same titles of privilege referred to in Exodus 19:3-6 to the new people of God, the church. Hosea, chapters 1 and 2 and Romans

9:25-26, should also be studied in conjunction with 1 Peter 2:9-10. Both Peter and Paul apply the prophecy concerning Loammi (No People) and Loruhamah (No Mercy) to the church! We are indeed the children of promise.

If our descendants are to be as the stars of the heavens and as the dust of the earth, there is still much room for growth. The nations of the world desperately need to be blessed by God through us. I know of no class of Scripture passages which so strongly undergird as many types of church growth as these. Certainly they speak to numerical, conceptual, expansion, extension, and bridging growth.

8. Its Cargo of Presuppositions

One of the large ships which sails the church growth river is loaded with a cargo of presuppositions. Those presuppositions may help us to understand church growth theory and practice. They might even help us to positionize ourselves within the movement, or against it. That cargo is stored in four compartments marked "Biblical Presuppositions," "Theological Presuppositions," "Anthropological Presuppositions," and "Attitudinal Presuppositions."

Spacewise, the biblical cargo is in a small area. Yet, that area is the passageway which leads directly into the much larger compartments containing the other cargo.

Biblical Presuppositions

Church growth presupposes that a "biblical theological position is the bedrock of church growth." Whatever theology church growth espouses, it is assumed that that theology will be based on the Bible, that it will be a biblical theology.

Second, the "typical church-growth advocate is thoroughly committed to the doctrines of the inspiration and authority of Scripture."[1] The Scriptures are believed to be inspired by God, "utterly trustworthy, the only infallible rule of faith and practice."[2]

Third, church growth presupposes that "plain biblical statements" should be taken at their face value.[3] Church growth advocates do have a high view of Scripture. One problem, however, with taking plain biblical statements at face value is: what do you do when there are several equally valid interpretations of the same statement? Moreover, how can you be sure any statement is not distorted by your own grid?[4]

We never come to the Bible with minds which are like blank tablets. Costas, therefore, scores church growth theorists for having a shallow hermeneutic. By that he means that they have not contended in depth with the problem which arises out of the space-time difference between the biblical text and their historical situation.[5]

It is ironical that church growth theorists, with all of their emphasis on culture, research, and the use of the behavioral sciences, have not exhibited a comparable concern for the critical study of the Bible. "They have failed," says Costas, "to use the same scientific tools to interpret the text in the light of the many situations of contemporary man."[6]

Theological Presuppositions

When we enter into that compartment labeled "Theological Presuppositions," it is at first a bit difficult for us to make out these items in the dimly lit cargo compartment of the ship. As we move closer, all of the traditional doctrines presupposed by conservative, evangelical Christians appear to be there. We see those presuppositions about the deity of Christ, the person and work of the Holy Spirit, belief in the lostness of humanity apart from faith in Jesus Christ, belief in heaven and hell, and so forth.

Closer inspection reveals that this is indeed the first theological presupposition, the assumption by church growth theorists that "we have an adequate theology which we have received from the past."[7]

Nevertheless, our guide shows us that there are some distinctive theological presuppositions which have been hammered out by church growth people. One of these is that God is interested in results. Ultimately, evangelistic and missionary effectiveness have to be measured by disciples, not by decisions. Numerical church growth is a crucial task in missions. "The church that does not grow," says Glasser, "is out of the will of God."[8]

Wagner was once asked: "What one characteristic describes church growth more than any other?" His answer essentially was: "We are kind of the Weight Watchers of churches, but we try to help them put on weight, not to take it off."[9] Church growth presupposes that churches ought to put on weight—the weight of new, countable disciples and new, countable churches.

A third theological presupposition is that churches should concentrate on the responsive elements of society. "One of our basic assumptions," says McGavran, "is that God prepares certain people to accept His Son."[10] Win the winnable while they are winnable is church growth advice. Don't neglect or abandon resistant people, but concentrate available resources on receptive people. McGavran puts it in a kind of aphorism: "Gospel acceptors should always have a higher priority than Gospel rejectors."[11]

A fourth theological presupposition is that conversion is not necessarily an individual decision. Church growth prefers to call it a "multiindividual, mutually-interdependent decision." Nearly three billion persons belong to the Fourth World of lost persons. Over two billion of these live in people groups within which there are no Christians. Near-neighbor evangelism will not touch them. E-3 and E-2 evangelism may. Even so, they cannot be picked off one by one. Church growth believes that if such persons are to be reached, it must be through people movements such as the residents of Lydda and Sharon in Acts 9:35.

A fifth of these presuppositions is that discipling and perfecting can be separated, although they are closely interrelated. McGavran divides Matthew 28:19-20 into two parts. The first part he calls discipling and the second perfecting. "A people is discipled," contends McGavran, "when its individuals feel united around Jesus Christ as Lord and Saviour, believe themselves to be members of His Church, and realize that 'our folk are Christians, our book is the Bible, and our house of worship is the church.' " Perfecting is the "bringing about of an ethical change in the discipled group, an increasing achievement of a thoroughly Christian way of life for the community as a whole, and the conversion of the individuals making up each generation as they come to the age of decision."[12]

More recently McGavran has sought to clarify his thought on discipling and perfecting by identifying three meanings of the verb *disciple.* These are represented by the symbols D1, D2, and D3. D1 is when a non-Christian society, under the influence of the Holy Spirit, become baptized and committed Christians. D2 is the initial conversion of individuals in a nominally Christian society. D3 is when an individual Christian becomes an informed, illuminated, thoroughly dedicated follower of Jesus Christ.

McGavran brings his clarification to a head in these revealing words: "Discipling Two and Discipling Three are attractive new terms. In individualistic American society, in a land where becoming Christian did not mean 'leaving one's own people and joining another people,' D2 and D3 were desirable processes. Consequently, church growth men and others started using the word 'discipling' in the second and third meanings. I myself, in my writing to Americans and my advocacy of American church growth, have used the new verb in senses two and three."[13]

A sixth theological presupposition is that Christian growth may be based on a biological-educational model of conversion. McGavran's three levels of discipling point to such a model. The ideal in discipling is D3, but apparently one never begins there. The pilgrimage begins with D1 or D2. Moreover, by dichotomizing the Great Commission into discipling and perfecting, a biological-educational model is necessitated. The traumatic, Damascus Road model of Saul of Tarsus would not fit too neatly into church growth theory.

Mennonite Robert L. Ramseyer sums up the theological implications of the biological-educational model: "The new Christian must be led gradually from his first commitment to Christ to a state of maturity in which he will come to understand more fully the implication of that commitment for his way of life. This growth model applies both to individual Christians and to churches. On this basis church growth theory is able to separate church planting and Christian living, discipling and perfecting, mission and applied Christianity."[14]

A seventh presupposition, which can be more easily understood in the light of the above, is that priority is given to evangelism over all other activities and functions of the church. Church growth self-consciously gives evangelism top billing. Evangelism is making disciples. God's imperative in the Great Commission is to make disciples. Moreover, "Disciples are tangible, identifiable, countable people," says Wagner, "and whenever a true disciple is made, church growth occurs."[15]

McGavran's prioritizing of evangelism may be clearly seen in a letter which he wrote to the editor of *Sojourners* magazine in 1977. Commenting on the many good works of *Sojourners* in the light of the three billion who do not believe on Jesus Christ, McGavran says: "Such action is *good* but is *not* enough. The most desperate need of the three billion is a knowledge of the loving, righteous God, his commands, and his plan for the redemption of men and women. What the three billion need, in order to find within themselves justice flowing down like waters, is *millions of churches* . . . . Nothing, but nothing, will more rapidly dissipate the grievous ills of mankind."[16]

Wagner goes so far as to differentiate between social service and social action. He believes it is all right for churches to do social service, but not social action. "I hesitate," says Wagner, "to classify social action as any priority for churches as churches at all."[17]

This presupposition about prioritizing evangelism over social service, social action, and all else, is given an interesting twist by one of McGavran's fellow churchmen. William J. Richardson of Northwest Christian College argues that evangelism is social action and that Christianization is humanization.[18]

The eighth and last of these theological presuppositions has to do with obedience. Church growth leaders insist on obedience to the Word of God and to the will of God. Their aim is to please God and not men. They are true believers. If they should appear adamant and unbending at times, it may be due to their heartfelt desire to be found faithful to their Lord.

Anthropological Presuppositions

A third compartment in this ship loaded with a heavy cargo of presuppositions is labeled "Anthropological Presuppositions." These are mostly assumptions which relate to the cultures of mankind.

The first, and most far-reaching, of these presuppositions is that the clash between Christianity and the many cultures of mankind "is confined to one or two percent of the components." McGavran says "there is no clash with ninety-five percent of these components." What clash there is has to do with the gods, fetishes, charms, in short "the paraphernalia of idolatry and spirit worship," and with such practices as head-hunting.[19]

All of that means "Christianity is wholly neutral to the vast majority of cultural components." McGavran identifies his point of view as having much similarity with Richard Niebuhr's Christ the transformer of culture model.[20]

Church growth spokesmen presuppose that receptivity to the Christian faith is to a large extent dependent upon social and cultural factors.[21] McGavran, while commenting on another matter, puts it this way: "Contrary to the presuppositions of many, some causes of growth are nontheological."[22] Indeed, this is a second anthropological presupposition.

"Church growth," McGavran contends, "often depends on harvesting fields when they are ripe."[23] Bishop Waskom Pickett's pioneering research on *Christian Mass Movements in India* reveals that many Indians came to Christ for social reasons.[24]

A third of these anthropological presuppositions has to do with the rate of change as it relates to receptivity to the gospel. It is presupposed that those populations undergoing change will be more receptive to the Christian faith. Particularly would this apply to those tribal or pretribal societies which may be moving from animism to some other belief system, those repressed people called the masses in more complex societies, and urban people who have recently left the countryside.

The presupposition about change also applies to such changes as loss of a mate through death or divorce, changing residences, taking a new job, and so forth. It is assumed that openness to change may be equated with openness to the gospel.[25]

A fourth presupposition, which follows directly in the above chain, is that the most important subunit in cultures is the homogeneous unit because "the gospel flows best over living bridges, the channels of family and friendship."[26] That presupposition enables McGavran to utter what might be called a trumpet sound: "The Church should ride the chariot of lineage and clan to a discipling of the tribes."[27]

The vast amount of church growth literature which treats such items as "people movements," "group conversion," and "multiindividual mutually-interdependent decision," "the homogeneous unit," and so forth, should be tied to this crucial presupposition. The language may be a bit foreign to us. Nevertheless, the presupposition applies to individualistic Western cultures as well as to Third World cultures.

A fifth presupposition is that the social sciences should be used in researching church growth. Anthropology, sociology, psychology, communications theory, statistical analysis, and so forth, all have a role to play in church growth. These sciences are considered neutral in themselves. Church growth leaders want to see them used to determine the causes of church growth and nongrowth. So far, it is fair to say that these sciences have been used as tools rather than as exact sciences.[28]

Another of these presuppositions is that the use of a medical model yields considerable mileage in conveying the substance and intention of church growth. Thus, a healthy church grows. One may have "church growth eyes," discern the body, and so forth. There is a "disease of slow-growth." Wagner takes this medical model to its greatest length in his volume, *Your Church Can Be Healthy.*[29] Eight church growth diseases, two of them fatal, are treated by Wagner.

Still a seventh presupposition is that church growth requires detailed and long-range planning. Church growth theorists are not opposed to applying Management by Objectives (MBO) in their work. McGavran is bold to advocate planning as much as fifty years in advance.

Attitudinal Presuppositions

The last cargo compartment on our imaginary ship is filled with attitudinal presuppositions. Church growth is an attitude, a mood, a mind-set. Our last compartment is not large in size, but is large in significance.

Church growth advocates presuppose a pragmatic attitude toward methods, a positive attitude toward results, and an optimistic attitude toward the future. Pragmatism, positivism, and optimism characterize both its theoreticians and its practitioners.

A pragmatic attitude toward method is presupposed. There are no sacred methods. George W. Peters expresses the idea thusly: "There is only *one gospel* but many methods. The gospel is absolute, final, complete, perfect; *it is revelation given.* Not so the methods; they are conditioned by time, culture and psychology. Methods are relative. *They are people-related.* The Bible, therefore, does not lay down absolute patterns in methods."[30]

Church growth is fiercely pragmatic. It is skeptical of claims which can't be substantiated with facts. It takes no method at face value. It doesn't waste much time thinking about what should bring persons to Christ. Rather it is more concerned with what does bring people to Christ.[31]

To church growth theorists the goal is more important than the means. The questions they are forever asking about means are: "Will it work?" and "What is working?"

Church growth presupposes a positive attitude toward results. The seed we sow in church growth may not bring forth a Baptist body, but it will bring forth some part of the body of Christ. McGavran writes: "As long as the evangelization of the world seems vague, ill-managed, and impossible, it attracts relatively little money and few men."[32] Is it any wonder that John R. Mott, who coined that phrase "The Evangelization of the World in This Generation," wrote the foreword for the 1938 edition of McGavran's *Church Growth and Group Conversion?* [33]

McGavran is positive that "More winnable people live in the world today than ever before."[34] For example, "Africa south of the Sahara is even now in the midst of a march to Christ so huge that by the year 2000 there will be well over 200 million Christians there—David Barrett estimates there will be 357 million."[35]

This positive attitude toward results bleeds through in Ralph D. Winter's account of what he calls *The 25 Unbelievable Years 1945-1969:*

> The church in Korea grew more in the years 1953-60 than it had in the previous sixty years. The church in Sub-Sahara Africa more than tripled from thirty to ninety-seven million. In Indonesia at least fifty thousand Moslems became Christians—the first time in history that such a turning from Islam had taken place. The South India Conference of the Methodist Church in the face of persecution grew from 95,000 to 190,000 members. The Presbyterian Church in Taiwan between 1955 and 1965 engaged in a "Double the Church Campaign" and concluded it successfully. In Latin America, largely due to ceaseless and effective personal evangelism on the part of the Pentecostal family of Churches, Protestants grew from about 1,900,000 in 1945 to at least 19,000,000 in 1970. In Brazil alone, by 1970, new congregations of the evangelical variety were being founded at the rate of three thousand per year.[36]

Probably no one in America best exemplifies this positive attitude toward results than Robert H. Schuller. Schuller's church for a number of years grew at a decadal growth rate of over 500 percent.[37] Schuller's book, *Your Church Has Real Possibilities,* spells out what he means by "possibility thinking."[38]

As a concommitant to the pragmatism and positivism, church growth thinkers also presuppose an optimistic attitude toward the future. One of their favorite texts is "I will build my church, and the powers of death shall not prevail against it" (Matt. 16:18b). McGavran says, "The missionary movement has just begun." He has little patience with "the pygmy complex."[39]

An early issue of the Church Growth Bulletin expresses this optimism in these strong terms: "The Christian Church stands at the beginning of her mission. The minor church growth of the nineteenth and twentieth centuries is only the prologue. The great turning to Christ and the mighty multiplication of His churches lie ahead. The era of church plantings has only just begun."[40]

McGavran's unforgettable expression of this irrepressible optimism is that we are in the "sunrise, not the sunset of mission."[41] If the nineteenth century was "the great century" in church growth, the twentieth century is destined to be even greater. For church growth advocates, the best seems always yet to be.

9. Its Cargo of Principles

The largest ships which ply the church growth river are those which haul its principles. Like all ships which move up and down the rivers of the world, these ships fly the flag of their respective country. They are indigenous as it were. Yet, some of these ships fly an international flag. They may belong to the United Nations, rather than to a particular nation.

These two kinds of flags, so prominently displayed on all ships, yield an analogy relating to church growth principles. Some church growth principles are international, universally owned, and applicable almost everywhere. Other church growth principles are indigenous to particular cultures, locally owned, and not necessarily applicable elsewhere.

The glossary in McGavran and Arn's *Ten Steps for Church Growth* defines a church growth principle as "a worldwide truth which, when properly applied, along with other principles, contributes significantly to the growth of the church."[1] There are three major parts to that definition: (1) a church growth principle is called a *worldwide* truth; (2) it should be properly applied in concert with other principles; and (3) if so, it will contribute significantly to the growth of the church.

That definition is fine except for the qualifying adjective "worldwide" in part 1. Not all church growth principles are worldwide. Some are, but some are not. McGavran himself recognizes this in his chapter on "Indigenous Church Principles and Growing Churches." "Since the Church in every land ought to be a Church of that land and that culture, and since our Lord uses missionaries from one land to plant the Gospel in others, the essential question is this: How can a foreign missionary multiply churches of Jesus Christ rather than pale copies of the ones that sent him out? How can missionaries multiply churches which are Spirit-filled and thoroughly of the people? In China, truly Chinese? In Bolivia, thoroughly Bolivian? Among the upper classes, genuinely upper-class, and among the masses, genuinely of the masses?"[2]

Ramseyer is therefore correct when he observes that "church growth theory does not lay down principles for evangelization and church building which are applicable in *any* situation."[3] Part of the confusion on this point arises from the church growth school itself. Alongside church growth principles in the same glossary is the listing of "Biblical Principles." The latter are defined as "truths revealed in Scripture, founded on revelation, and believed as bedrock to the faith."[4]

Therefore, the first point I wish to make about church growth principles is that they are not necessarily worldwide truths which are forever universally applicable. To whatever extent they are truly biblical principles, that is, "truths revealed in Scripture" and "founded on revelation," they may be called worldwide truths.

A second point should be made about principles by way of introduction. They may be, and indeed are, contrasted with methods. Isn't there a bit of doggerel which says something to the effect: "Methods are many, principles are few. Methods frequently change; but principles never do"?

While principles may not be few in church growth, they are fewer than church growth methods. While it may not be true that church growth principles never change, they do change less frequently than church growth methods. Wagner expresses this strongly when he points out that church growth maintains: "A ruthlessly objective attitude toward evangelistic methods. Methods simply cannot be 'canned' in Lower Zax . . . and exported to Mamba Bamba. Church growth diligently seeks to locate, describe, and analyze for each time and place, the methods that God has blessed and those he has not blessed."[5]

Hence, principles are both more "exportable" and "importable" than are methods. Methods are even more indigenous than principles.

A third handle for getting hold of church growth principles is to see them in terms of their adjectival meanings, namely "most important, main, chief." Often in the church growth literature principles which are lifted up are the mainstays of church growth—the chief supports which hold up the church growth structure, the most important pilings in the whole church growth foundation.

If you can think of the cargo of church growth principles (1) as "not necessarily" worldwide truths universally and eternally applicable; (2) as over against church growth methods; and (3) as the main supports in the church growth structure, you will be able to handle them with greater facility. They will also make better sense to you.

Prior to examining the cargo of church growth principles, one more question needs to be raised. Are these principles applicable to all sizes of churches? There are approximately 330,000 churches in the United States of America. Add another 20,000 for Canada. Not many of those 350,000 churches are very large numerically. In fact, Lyle Schaller says 50 percent of all churches in America average from 15 to 75 worshiping members; 30 percent average from 75 to 200; 15 percent average from 200 to 350; and 5 percent average from 350 to 2,000. The number of churches averaging over 2,000 worshiping members is between 100 and 200, too small a percentage to count.[6]

Therefore, if the principles do not apply to small churches, we are not talking to at least 50 percent, and possibly 80 percent of the churches. All of the principles will doubtlessly not apply to all of the churches. Yet, enough of them will probably apply to your church, regardless of its size, to help you become a more effective growth agent. If your church is still tarrying in the "courtyard of non-growth,"[7] you may be especially benefited by inspecting this cargo of principles.

The Process Principle

Church growth is a process, not an event![8] This is a simple yet profound truth. Many churches and denominations are *event* oriented rather than *process* oriented. In church growth there may be many events, but no one event or two events will produce sustained church growth.

Consider the following implications of the process principle:

1. Because church growth is a process rather than an event; it requires planning—long-range planning, annual planning, and day-to-day planning.
2. Because church growth is a process, it requires management of time, programs, personnel, materials, and so forth. The business world refers to this as MBO (Management by Objectives).
3. Because church growth is a process rather than an event, it involves setting objectives and goals and specific actions which can be measured and calendared.
4. Because church growth is a process, it is dynamic rather than static. It is flexible and fluid rather than set in concrete. It is forever changing and evolving.
5. Because church growth is a process, it interacts dynamically with culture. It never occurs in a cultural vacuum.
6. Because church growth is a process, it is not a gimmick. It is not a clever scheme to lift a church out of a numerical slump. It doesn't seek to "hook" persons through some cleverly devised manipulations of their psyche. Church

growth exists for long-term gains and not just for short-term results.

7. Because church growth is a process, it must have a healthy respect for history. It takes the long look backward and forward. It sees the spiritual value of accurate records.

8. Because church growth is a process, it is not a fad here today and gone tomorrow. There can be nothing effervescent about church growth. McGavran is only the father of the *modern* church growth movement. Even so, he has been working at it diligently for well over twenty years. If it were a fad, it might have flourished and perished twenty deaths in that many years. God, the heavenly Father, is really the Father of all genuine church growth.

9. Because church growth is a process, it is not a program which you can pick up this fall and lay down next summer. Programs come and go, but a process starts and continues until its completion. You can't pick it up and lay it aside at your pleasure without suffering dire consequences.

The process principle is one of the most important, basic, and far-reaching of all church growth principles. It interfaces with all of the other principles. If there is a "worldwide truth" in church growth, this is surely one of them.

The Pyramid Principle

David Womack of the Assemblies of God defines the pyramid principle for us: "The Pyramid Principle states that for a church to grow it must expand its base of organization and ministry before it may add to its mass of followers." Womack expands that: "When we speak of church growth, then, we mean something more than numerical increase. We also mean the expanded development of the ministry and administration of the church to care for a given number of people."[9]

Womack uses the analogy of the pyramids in Egypt

and among the Mayas of South America to illustrate the pyramid principle. The concept of the pyramid was one of the most creative ideas of all time. It apparently began with Imhotep, history's first engineer and constructor in stone.

There are apparent examples of pyramids which began on a certain scale and then were enlarged. However, before the mass of those pyramids could be enlarged, their bases had to be expanded to accommodate the larger mass. In fact, to make a pyramid larger, you must enlarge its base and then add to its mass. So it is with the church.

The pyramid principle is another way of saying that quantitative growth must be balanced with qualitative growth. If McGavran's four types of church growth were called upon to illustrate the principle, we would say that expansion, extension, and bridging growth must be balanced with internal growth. If the Costas types of growth were used to illustrate the principle, we would say that numerical growth must be balanced with organic growth.

What concerns Womack is the "doubling time" of a church. He thinks "a healthy, growing church should maintain a long-term doubling time of 4 to 6 years, with occasional thrusts of 2 to 4 years."[10] When doubling does occur, Womack says the application of the pyramid principle will prevent the increased mass of followers from toppling over due to an insufficient base of organization and ministry.

Thomas A. Wolf, pastor of The Church on Brady, a growing Southern Baptist congregation in Los Angeles, expresses the pyramid principle in terms of a contrast between a "pyramid of paralysis" and a "pyramid of power." If you keep adding members to your congregation without correspondingly adding to your organizational and leadership base, you are building a pyramid of paralysis. However, if you simultaneously enlarge your organizational and leadership base while you are adding many new disciples to your church, you are building a pyramid of power.[11]

Some fast-growing churches are building a pyramid of paralysis. Unless such churches learn to apply the pyramid principle, they may soon reach a point of no growth. Like Humpty Dumpty they may experience a great fall, and somebody else will have to come along and pick up the pieces.

I think what more often happens to Humpty Dumpty churches is that they minister to a passing parade. They reach and baptize a multitude of persons, but they teach and train only a handful of those reached. Again, this is a clear violation of the pyramid principle. Such churches are building a pyramid of paralysis rather than a pyramid of power.

DuBose is very strong on the pyramid principle without using the term. When he discusses "The Balance Principle" and calls for balance in the application of two of three of his other principles, he is calling for what Womack wants in his pyramid principle, and for what Wolf wants in his pyramid of power.[12]

The closest thing Southern Baptists have to the pyramid principle is the "Growth Spiral." Created by Andy Anderson, the Growth Spiral is "a tool for helping a church set quarterly goals for growth in Sunday School enrollment, teaching units and the number of persons participating in visitation."[13]

A more popular name for the "Growth Spiral" is the "Church Growth Spiral." It is an expansion of the basic laws of Sunday School growth, especially of what is generally referred to as the Flake Formula. Arthur Flake, a pioneer Sunday School leader among Southern Baptists, taught a five-point formula for Sunday School growth.

The Flake Formula says: (1) locate the prospects; find out who and where they are; (2) enlarge the organization;

set up the necessary classes and other units in your organization to accommodate these prospects; (3) enlist and train the necessary teachers and other leaders to teach these prospects; (4) provide the necessary space for these new units and new teachers; (5) go after the prospects in an aggressive visitation program; reach them through these new teachers and units and space.

The Church Growth Spiral is an extension and enlargement of the Flake Formula. The typical spiral projects quarterly growth goals for a period of two years. Moreover, it projects that growth in a *balanced* manner. All five points of the formula are held in balanced tension with each other. Furthermore, the spiral relates these five factors to worship attendance, stewardship of money, and baptism.

The most perfect tool Southern Baptists have for applying the pyramid principle is Andy Anderson's Church Growth Spiral. Anderson says the spiral can assist the churches in five ways: (1) "it accelerates growth, both in quantity and quality"; (2) "it can be a tool for improving the quality of the Sunday School organizations"; (3) "it helps a church to establish a visitation program"; (4) it "aids long-range planning"; and, (5) it "results in more persons accepting Christ and, therefore, more baptisms."[14]

The Receptivity Principle

Priority in church growth should be given to those who are most receptive to the gospel. We should put our greatest resources where they will provide the largest harvest now. McGavran calls this "Winning the winnable while they are winnable."[15] George Hunter is convinced that the "Church Growth movement's greatest contribution to this generation's world evangelization will be its stress upon receptivity."[16]

Hence, church growth presents us with a priority of

priorities! Top priority is to be given to evangelism. Within that priority foremost attention is to be given to winning the winnable. Gospel acceptors are to have priority over gospel rejectors.

Whether you agree with the receptivity principle or not, you will want to understand it. Here is the way McGavran reasons: "Since the Gospel is to be preached to all creation, no Christian will doubt but that both the receptive and the resistant should hear it. And since gospel acceptors have an inherently higher priority than gospel rejectors, no one should doubt that, whenever it comes to a choice between reaping ripe fields or seeding others, the former is commanded by God."[17]

McGavran assumes that "the masses are growing increasingly responsive" to the gospel, and that "particular masses in certain countries and sections of countries fluctuate in response" to the gospel. His opinion is that it should not be a matter of policy "to beseige indifferent and resistant or even rebellious segments of any type."[18]

If McGavran is right, the poor and repressed, the forgotten and the oppressed, are the most receptive persons in our world to the gospel. They are the most responsive because they are most open to change.

Charles Arn puts it this way: "A well-tested principle of church growth is that 'Unchurched people are most responsive to a change in life-style . . . during periods of transition.' " These periods of transition might be times when an individual or a people have their normal behavior patterns disrupted by some unusual event which requires an unfamiliar response.[19]

Examples of such events might be marriage, divorce, birth, and hospitalization. A newly married couple is more open to change because the couple is in a state of transition. Following a divorce, persons are also in a state of transition and more open to a change in their life-style. The same is true when a family member is hospitalized, or when a new baby is born to a couple.

A receptivity-rating scale has actually been worked out listing forty-one different events, in approximate order of their importance, that precipitate personal or family transition. Ranked at the very top of that scale is the death of a spouse. At the bottom is a minor violation of the law. Other high-ranking transition events are divorce, marital separation, jail term, death of close family member, and personal injury or illness. Even events such as a spouse starting to work or a change in living conditions are transition events which make one more open to a change in life-style.

Those who have "church growth eyes" will see these times of transition as opportunities for outreach. They will perceive that the longer the time lapse following such transitions, the less receptive the person or family will be. Also, they will know that these events may compound each other and thus create greater openness.[20]

Illustrations of the receptivity principle may be multiplied in the conversion of persons while they were away from home. Examples in the book of Acts are: the Cypriot Barnabas, the Ethiopian eunuch, Saul of Tarsus, the Italian centurion Cornelius, Lydia of Thyatira, and Apollos of Alexandria.

Look also at the Japanese. Less than 1 percent of the Japanese in Japan profess Christ. Even though the Japanese have had a professing Christian at the helm of their nation, not much church growth has occurred there in more than 100 years of missions. Yet a study was reported in 1977 which showed that 43 percent of the more than 700,000 Japanese living in Brazil profess some form of Christianity even though 98 percent of those who immigrated were non-Christian.

Even if we narrow that figure down to those who actively practice their faith, there is a minimum of 8 percent within the circle of faith, an astounding 800 percent above that in their homeland. A similar contrast might be made between the Chinese of the homeland in the Peoples' Republic of China and the Chinese of the dispersion in Taiwan. Apparently minority dispersion people are more responsive to the gospel than those in staunchly resistant homelands.[21]

The receptivity principle may appear to us to be more applicable in other countries than here at home. It may appear to be more applicable to bridging and extension growth than to expansion growth. Such appearances are deceitful. The mission field is everywhere. All types of church growth are needed *in* our country. Much of the world has come to us. There are both receptive and resistant persons in every country. One reason some churches aren't growing is that they are not harvesting the ripe fields.

One final aspect of the receptivity principle is its interaction with the church's communication. DuBose refers to what he calls "the Principle of Impact—Penetration Balance." "In an urban society," says DuBose, "more communication is needed for impact, and a small group communication is needed for penetration."[22]

Receptivity to the gospel is greater among those who have been impacted with it. Costas seems to pick up on this point when he criticizes the inadequate "confrontation with communication theory" in McGavran, Tippett, and others.[23] Since then, Engel and Norton have taken some of the sting out of that criticism.[24]

Engel has continued to develop a communications model which is sometimes called "Engel's Evangelistic Countdown." Engel calls his model "The Spiritual-Decision Process." The model is scaled on a continuum "running from complete lack of awareness of the Gospel to abundant knowledge about it." The main point which Engel wishes to make is that: "We are too prone to refer to a person, to a group, or to an entire field as closed to evangelism, when, in reality, our communication has been off target."[25]

Ralph Neighbor of Houston, Texas, has developed a much simpler communications model. He calls it "The Way People Come to Christ." The model is conceptualized in the form of a pyramid. The base of that pyramid is called "UNAWARENESS," and assigned no number. Conversely, the narrow cone of the pyramid is called "Characterization—Growth in Christ," and assigned the number 6. As one moves up the pyramid, it is evident that one cannot be receptive to Christ as Lord and Savior until step 5.[26]

Thus DuBose, Engel, and Neighbor sound a word of caution to those who would push the receptivity too far. Communications theory need not contradict the principle, but it should cause us to examine our communication before too hastily writing off persons as resistant and unresponsive.

The New Unit Principle

Much as the fruit of a grapevine is produced on the new growth, so the fruit of church growth comes from new units—new members, new churches, new missions, new associations, new state conventions, new denominations, new Sunday Schools, new departments, new classes, new units of almost any kind and description. Growth always comes on the new growth.

Chaney and Lewis are very strong on the new unit principle. "New unit growth," writes Chaney and Lewis, "is the only area in which *significant church growth* will take place in the next twenty-five years." By new units Chaney and Lewis mean new people, new organizational units such as Bible study classes, and new extension and bridging units such as missions and churches.[27]

Not all new units are designed for outward growth.

Those that are can be counted on to present new problems. They may bring in different kinds of persons. Financial pressure will come. New units will create leadership and personal problems. Space and staff problems may surface.

However, the other side of that ledger, according to Chaney and Lewis, is that "new people integrated into an organization bring growth. New units that enlarge the organization bring growth. New organizational units that offer a variety of ministries bring growth. New space in which the organization may function brings growth. New leadership in the organization can produce growth."[28]

A research experiment funded by the Lilly Foundation, supports the new unit principle. Two groups of ministers and churches were compared in the research. One group was told not to replace Sunday School teachers who resigned during the year, but to combine that class with another class of about the same age to make one larger class. The other group was told: "In every children's department with two or more classes, add another teacher and another class. Then reassign the existing pupils to give all classes an equal enrollment."

What happened? "Attendance in every combined class of the first experimental group had declined noticeably, and was now no larger than it had been at the beginning of the experiment." In the second group, "by the end of the first year, all the classes that were divided had grown back to the size of the original classes." These churches also increased total Sunday School attendance, and showed a subsequent increase in church members.[29]

Any church which is serious about expansion growth must continuously begin new outreach units. New Bible study cells, classes, departments, and divisions are especially needed. Some churches need to start dual and even triple Sunday Schools in order to grow. Backyard Bible study groups and home Bible study groups need to be started by the hundreds and thousands.

New missions and mission-type churches need to be multiplied all over the land, among the myriads of homogeneous groups in America. New units which will be "need oriented" should be multiplied. Find a need and meet it through a new outreach unit. Meet people at their points of need. Significant growth will never occur in the old, existing units until they are thoroughly pruned. Often the pruning of old units is more painful than the starting of new ones.

The Homogeneous Principle

"Men like to become Christians," writes McGavran, "without crossing social, linguistic, or class barriers."[30] McGavran and Arn define a homogeneous unit as "a group of people who all have some characteristic in common and feel that they 'belong.' "[31]

Biblical barriers such as "the cross, the need to repent, to be baptized, to give up known sin . . . must remain," says McGavran. It is the nonbiblical barriers which must not be erected. These are barriers such as education, wealth, employment, and ethnic sections of a city such as Italian, Irish, and German sections. Such homogeneous units must be respected and such differences must be used for the glory of God, McGavran thinks. McGavran leaves no doubt where he stands in regard to the homogeneous unit principle: "We must make sure that we ask people to become Christian where they don't have to cross barriers of language and culture and class and wealth and style of life. Every man should be able to become a Christian with his own kind of people."[32]

People will go to church where they feel at home and where they feel that they belong. The homogeneous unit principle realistically recognizes this sociological fact of life.

When you raise the question, "How do churches empirically grow?" Wagner acknowledges that to be a sociological question. He admits that is not a sufficient reason for a Christian to hold to the principle. Wagner feels that the principle is defensible even on biblical, theological, and ethical grounds. "My position," says Wagner, "is that culture is not sinful," although every culture has demonic elements in it. Wagner argues that "Jesus started no Gentile church." He points out that eleven of the first twelve apostles were Aramaic-speaking Galilean Jews. Judas Iscariot was the exception, and Matthias, an Aramaic-speaking Jew, was elected to replace Judas.

Wagner does concede two points: (1) "the homogeneous unit principle is a starting point. If it's an ending point, it is sub-Christian." (2) He concedes that there are certain "social disaster areas" in today's world where the homogeneous unit principle should perhaps be violated. One such disaster area might be South Africa. "They might have to sacrifice growth temporarily in order to combat the racism of that country," Wagner thinks.[33]

Orjala is very positive toward the homogeneous unit principle. He agrees that America is not a melting pot so much as it is a stewing pot, that 43.4 percent of Americans are unmelted ethnics.

Orjala seeks to popularize much of what McGavran and Wagner say about the HU. "The spread of the gospel has followed the lines of homogeneous units from the very beginning," says Orjala. He illustrates that by pointing to John 1:35-46. "This is quite a chain reaction! It starts first of all with the homogeneous unit of a *religious group,* John the Baptist and his disciples. Next, the witness travels through a *kinship* homogeneous unit, the brothers Andrew and Peter. Then a *locality* group is the focus—Andrew and Peter's credibility with Philip is used by Jesus. Finally, a *friendship* group comes into play with Philip and Nathanael."[34]

DuBose affirms the usefulness of the HU principle. Nevertheless, he insists that it must be applied in balance with what he calls "The Heterogeneous Principle." DuBose then proceeds with a devastating critique. Reacting in particular to McGavran's statement about how men *like* to become Christians without crossing barriers, DuBose says: "No man establishes the terms on which he will receive the gospel—the gospel establishes its own terms. The question is not what one *likes* to do to be saved but what one *must* do to be saved. The crux of the theological problem with this principle is that it operates on the assumption that the strongest ties which bind people are the human ties of culture. In the final analysis it treats evangelism like any other human transaction and the church like any other social organization. We ask the question: Where is the transcendent dimension?"[35]

We shall return to a critique of the HU principle in chapter 12. Presently, however, let us treat some of its commendable features and show how they relate to church growth here at home.

The HU principle helps us to see that persons "are not just individuals floating around in society, but they are individuals who are members of groups." Some of these HUs to which persons belong are *biological,* encompassing factors such as race, age, sex, and kinship. Some of these HUs have to do with *locality:* residence, origin, neighborhood, school, or work location. Some of the HUs are *cultural* in nature: language, social class, nationality, ethnic. Other HUs are *economic,* such as work, profession, trade (for example, blue collar, professional, clerical, unemployed). Still other HUs are *personal* and *social* encompassing special interests like hobbies, sports, and common experiences.

Taken together, this rich variety of HUs assist persons

with identity and belonging, credibility and protection, influence and control, and serve as a communication network.[36]

The homogeneous unit principle sees each of these HUs as a potential bridge across which the church can move into the world. Every HU is seen as a potential chariot through which the gospel rides into the lives of its members. One of the great contributions of church growth theory is that "men exist not as discrete individuals, but as inter-connected members of some society."[37]

The growth agent, local church, and denomination which can learn to mine the gold which is in the homogeneous unit principle, without sacrificing the pearl of great price which is the gospel, will experience fantastic church growth. America is a mosaic of homogeneous units. Almost every community is a mosaic of such units.

Southern Baptists are following the HU principle in their ethnic work. The Southern Baptist Convention probably ministers to more ethnics than any mainline Protestant church in America. There are over 1,400 SBC churches composed of more than thirty ethnic groups. On any given Sunday in California, Southern Baptists worship God in twenty-two different languages. There are over 500 black churches in the SBC. There are now probably more Spanish-speaking Baptist congregations in the United States than in all the rest of the world. Southern Baptists are probably the most integrated denomination in the world. However, it is extremely important to note that the integration has been achieved along the lines of HUs.[38]

Wagner uses Temple Baptist Church, located on Pershing Square in Los Angeles, to illustrate the HU principle. Temple has four congregations: an Anglo, Spanish, Chinese, and Korean congregation. That church is now aiming for at least two more congregations. They all are members of Temple Baptist. They all participate in the government of the church. Ordinarily the congregations worship separately in their own language. However, on the first Sunday of each quarter they all worship together in a celebration called "Sounds of Heaven."[39]

A steadfast refusal to recognize the validity of the HU principle cannot but impede church growth at home and abroad. What Tippett saw happen overseas could be duplicated in more subtle ways and on smaller scales here at home. Tippett testifies: "I have known some Western missionaries to refuse to harvest a field 'ripe unto harvest,' and even in one case to hold off people at gun-point when they came as a tribe to burn their fetishes and thus demonstrate their change of heart. These missionaries wanted them to come one by one, against their tribal cohesion."[40]

The Leadership Principle

Almost everybody who examines church growth concludes that the key of all keys, the master key as it were, is leadership. If a church has the right kind of leaders and the right amount of leaders, other factors being balanced, it will grow.

McGavran's five classes of leaders definitely fit into the leadership principle. Perhaps it will help us to briefly review those five classes and what McGavran means by them.

Class 1, voluntary leaders turned inward and primarily concerned with maintenance

Class 2, voluntary leaders turned outward and primarily concerned with outreach

Class 3, bivocational leaders who may be paid for part-time church work

Class 4, full-time, paid professionals such as pastors and other church staff members

Class 5, denominational workers whose work is primarily outside one local church

McGavran does not have in mind a hierarchy of leaders. Most churches are maintenance oriented in their leadership. They are asymmetrical when class 1 and class 2 leaders are compared. Some class 1 leaders double as class 2 leaders. Usually there are more class 1 than class 2. Until a church enlists, trains, and deploys more class 2 leaders, that church will not show much growth. All classes of leaders are necessary to the proper functioning of the church.

As you analyze your church, note especially the number of class 2 leaders in comparison to class 1 leaders. If your church is typical, you'll have very few class 2 leaders. Moreover, what class 2 leaders you do have may be doubling as class 1 leaders. Your church will not exhibit much balance between expansion and internal growth until you bring your class 2 leaders into better balance with your class 1s.

Now, look closely at your class 3 leaders. Do you have any? Perhaps your pastor is one. Perhaps your director of music is one. Do you have *any* part-time leaders who fall into this category? Some churches which consider themselves too small to have full-time staff members in Christian education, music, youth, recreation, and so forth, may have real potential for several part-time class 3 leaders. Particularly might some class 3 leaders aid your church with extension growth through servicing new missions and preaching points. One potential source of class 3 leaders which is frequently overlooked is persons who have retired from vocational Christian service.

Next, consider your class 4 leaders. What kind of longevity have they? Lyle Schaller puts it this way: "While there is no evidence to prove that long pastorates produce church growth, it is very rare to find a rapidly growing congregation that has had a series of short pastorates.''[41]

The December 1977 issue of *Home Missions* magazine surveyed the 425 fastest growing SBC churches, and concluded: "Only four percent of the churches have a pastor in his present position less than a year. Some 84 percent have been in their churches from one to ten years." Some 80 percent have been in the ministry more than ten years.[42]

Pastoral novices do not grow great churches. Pastors who are like rolling stones do not grow great churches. If you want to grow a great church, you should plan to plant your life in that church. An incarnational ministry is needed.

My family and I belong to the 194th fastest growing church in the SBC—Pleasant Valley Baptist Church, Route 2, Liberty, Missouri. Pastor Vernon Armitage has been with us nearly ten years, and so far as I know he plans to be with us indefinitely. It took Mr. Armitage two years to change the deacons from a board of directors and managers into a fellowship of ministers and servants. Up until 1978 we only had five deacons.

The church needs pastors who will consider their particular parishes a lifetime calling—pastors who are not looking around for greener pastures. The same is true for other full-time staff members. Peter Wagner says: "This principle of longevity does not apply only to the senior minister in a multiple staff church. In the healthiest situation it applies to everyone on the staff."[43]

While many local churches will have no class 5 leaders, they do need access to such leaders. No church is an island. Class 5 leaders are particularly important to bridging and extension growth. Moreover, it might be possible for a denomination to have too many class 5 leaders.[44] Especially is it important to examine the balance between outreach and inreach duties among class 5 leaders.

I am suggesting that intrinsic to McGavran's five classes of leaders is just about everything we need to analyze the leadership principle in a church or denomination, and indeed in the whole church. Another major aspect which we do need to touch upon are the qualities and characteristics of church growth leaders. Ron Lewis has lifted up eleven of these as follows:

1. The church growth leader should be a growing person. A growing church requires growing leaders.
2. The church growth leader knows the basic fundamentals of church growth.
3. The church growth leader has a *positive* life-style. He or she knows how to change minus signs into pluses.
4. The church growth leader has a deep respect for history. Church records are important.
5. The church growth leader looks to the future. The higher up the leadership pole he or she is, the longer chunk of time he or she will need to look at. For example, the pastor must take a longer look at the future than the Sunday School teacher.
6. The church growth leader must set priorities.
7. The church growth leader must be willing to take higher risks. The fruit of the tree is not at the trunk. It is out on the limb. When you put yourself out on a limb, there are always persons with hatchets who will chop at those limbs.
8. The church growth leader must have a high pain threshold.
9. The church growth leader must be patient, consistent, and insistent.
10. The church growth leader should have a world view. He or she must see beyond self and beyond the immediate and local.
11. The church growth leader must make a decision to *be,* no matter what happens. There is always resistence. Apart from a decision to be, the leader will be swept away like the chaff.[45]

Other Possible Principles

Among the numerous other possible church growth principles is one which might be called the accessibility and surplus parking principle. In a society which depends so much on the automobile, accessibility cannot be discussed apart from parking. Schuller is right: "It is obvious that the best product cannot be sold and will not be bought if people can't get their hands on it." Moreover, "Successful retailing demands SURPLUS parking!"[46] One reason many churches are not growing is that they do not have *surplus* parking. Even *adequate* parking will not allow for growth.

I can illustrate this principle in part by Moody Memorial Church in Chicago. This congregation was founded by D. L. Moody in the nineteenth century under another name. In 1925 and 1926 the present facilities were constructed on LaSalle Street in old Chicago. The structure cost one million dollars back then. Many of its members lived nearby. Now, most of its members are scattered. The auditorium seats 4,200 persons. But the average attendance on Sunday mornings is 1,400. The church has *no* parking. Public parking is at a minimum, especially during summer months as the church is located near Lincoln Park on Lake Michigan.

Hence, it is no accident that most of the fast-growing churches in America are located where persons can get to them easily. And when they do get to them, surplus parking will encourage them to come back.

We might also identify a methodological mix principle in church growth. McGavran and Arn define mix as "that combination of ingredients which taken together and in the right proportions produces effective church growth."[47]

What church growth people want is a mix of methods which will work to produce growth. That mix will be different for each church. What works for you may not work for another church.

The spiritual gift principle might also be mentioned. The principle says God has gifted every church and every Christian with the necessary spiritual gifts to enable body building. The classic biblical passage on this is Ephesians 4:7-16. Along with the Ephesians 4 passage there are three other primary passages on spiritual gifts: Romans 12:3-8; 1 Corinthians 12:1 to 14:40; and the lesser known passage of 1 Peter 4:7-11.

We might point out in passing that the Romans 12 passage connects the spiritual gifts with God; the Ephesians 4 passage connects them with the ascended Christ; and the Corinthians passage connects them with the Holy Spirit. Spiritual gifts therefore come from the Holy Trinity, God the Father, God the Son, and God the Holy Spirit.

Neither passage is complete. All the lists together are not exhaustive. They are, however, suggestive.

We probably owe the spiritual gift principle to classical and neo-Pentecostalism. We need not espouse what F. D. Brunner calls "subsequent experience theology"[48] and the belief that the sign equal to none that one has been baptized in the Holy Spirit is that he or she speaks with tongues, in order to affirm the principle of spiritual gifts.

Peter Wagner has written a book on this subject.[49] One chapter in his book is entitled, "The Myth of the Church Growth Pastor." Wagner says pulpit committees are looking for the "omnicompetent" pastor. Many Christians apparently think that every church growth pastor has the spiritual gifts of pastor, evangelist, and administration—or at least one or two of these three gifts. Not so, says Wagner. That's a myth. Some church growth pastors have none of these three gifts. The one thing, however, which all church growth pastors have in common is the ability to help others discover their spiritual gifts and to equip others to use their gifts.[50]

Wagner goes so far as to suggest that probably not more than 10 percent of the members in any one congregation have the gift of an evangelist. And by evangelist

Wagner means "the special ability that God gives to certain members of the body of Christ to share the Gospel with unbelievers in such a way that men and women become Jesus' disciples and responsible members of the church."[51]

According to Wagner, not every Christian is an evangelist; although every Christian is a witness. Wagner differentiates between the role of the witness and the gift of an evangelist. Wagner suggests five ways to help persons discover their spiritual gifts: explore the possibilities; experiment with as many as possible; examine your feelings; evaluate your effectiveness; and, expect confirmation from the body.[52]

The spiritual gifts principle fits the doctrine of the priesthood of the believer. It thrusts us into the layman's liberation movement—what Wagner calls "Laymen's Lib."[53] It reminds us that the Holy Spirit is the superintendent of the church.

10. Obstacles to Its Flow

Like all rivers, the church growth river has obstacles to its flow. There are mountains which must be cut through or bypassed. There are giant rocks and deep falls which create rapids in the stream. There may be occasional logjams. All kinds of debris may accumulate along the path of the life-giving water. Silt often gathers and collects. Even giant dams are erected in its path. Yet, the river flows on. Nothing can stop it permanently.

So many obstacles of such a large variety seek to obstruct the flow of the church growth river that we shall divide them into the three major classes of attitudinal, theological, and ecclesiastical. Overlapping and interfacing are so frequent among these obstacles that our classes of obstacles can only serve as magnets around which they tend to collect.

Attitudinal Obstacles

Seven attitudinal obstacles to the flow of the church growth river may be identified. Each of these may be caught up around a quotation.

It's up to them.[1] This attitude places the responsibility for church growth upon outsiders. It is the attitude which asks: "What's wrong with *them?* Why don't *they* come?" It is an attitude of *passivity.* Passive congregations are not growing congregations. A church can't open the usually locked doors of its beautiful sanctuary a few hours each week and expect to grow. As a Southerner might say: "You have to do more than unlock your doors on Sunday and say 'Y'all come.' "

Numbers are unimportant. There is an attitude that numbers are not really important, that faithfulness is the important thing. This attitude frequently sets quality over against quantity and faithfulness over against fruit.

McGavran in 1965 wrote: "Numbers of the redeemed are never 'mere.' They are important. They are treated as important in the New Testament."[2] Erich Voehringer, a Lutheran churchman, expands on the same idea: "The fewer Christians there are, the fewer potential witnesses. As long as we are in the flesh, we need numbers even in the church, knowing all the while that our statistics are as incomplete and unreliable as we are ourselves."[3]

Numbers can help us to quantify our problems and potential in church growth. They are correlatives to quality and faithfulness. We would do well to steer a middle course between those who have a neurosis for numbers and those who have a psychosis against numbers.

Small is beautiful. Closely akin to the attitude summed up under "Numbers are unimportant," the small is beautiful attitude is sometimes expressed as "big is bad." Peter Mankres in 1978 picked up on E. F. Schumacher's book, *Small Is Beautiful: Economics As If People Mattered,* and applied it to church growth. Mankres asserted: "The ministry of Christ frees us from the tyranny of statistics," and argued: "Value and size do not have a one-to-one correlation, either in the economic or the theological realm."[4]

Robert Hudnut in 1975 had argued along the same lines as Mankres. Hudnut wrote: "People are leaving the church. It could not be a better sign." His point was that "church growth is not the point." "If it grows," said Hudnut, "fine. If it doesn't grow, equally fine." "The point is whether the church is being true to the Gospel."[5] Neither Hudnut nor Mankres enters into any serious dialogue with the church growth movement.

A more balanced attitude might be that small is not necessarily beautiful, and big is not necessarily bad; the really beautiful thing is faithfulness to the Great Commission of our Lord to make disciples of all peoples. Persons full of prejudice favoring small churches, and full of fears against big churches are obstacles to church growth.

Any change is to be resisted. A consistently negative attitude toward all change is a great obstacle to church growth. All church growth entails change. There can be no growth without change. Steadfast resistance to change will keep your church from being blessed (or cursed) by the church growth river. Those who resent, and stiffly resist, change will perceive church growth as a threat and a curse. Those who want a Model T church in a Thunderbird world may feel constrained to stand as dikes against the swiftly flowing waters of the church growth river.

America is overchurched. Is it? We do have 330,000 churches. That's one church for about every 615 people. Yet, there are more than 80 million unchurched Americans. Moreover, many churches are dying, while many others are not growing as fast as the population.

Consider, for example, what is happening among Southern Baptists. Southern Baptists have averaged baptizing 1,000 persons per day for the last twenty-five years. They have averaged starting one church a day since 1845. In spite of that, in 1950 there was one Southern Baptist church for every 5,494 persons; whereas in 1972 there was one church for every 6,081 persons.[6] Southern Baptist growth is definitely not keeping pace with the population growth.

Wagner concludes that "three out of every four American adults are lost and need to be evangelized."[7] The blunt truth is that most of America's older churches are not growing. It isn't so much that members are dropping out of the churches. The problem is the decreasing numbers who join.[8] It appears that most of the growth for denominations comes through planting new churches. Probably what we need is *thousands* of new churches, but they must be churches organized to specifically reach the multitudes of different ethnic and homogeneous groups in our country. Furthermore, these new congregations should come into existence through planned parenthood.

Denominations are evil. Charles Clayton Morrison in the early 1950s blasted denominationalism in a book called *The Unfinished Reformation.* Morrison put his finger on the denomination as "the very nub of the problem of Christian unity." He formulated nine propositions against the denominational system. Morrison thought denominations "scandalously wasteful" and "a shameful embarrassment."[9]

Then, in 1973, Elmer Towns raised the question: *Is the Day of the Denomination Dead?*[10] Both Morrison and Towns favor the death of denominations, but for entirely different reasons. Morrison wanted them to die so the reformation could be finished with a new ecumenism. Towns wants them to die because he thinks the superaggressive churches can do a better job without the denominations.

The unvarnished truth is that the Protestant ecumenical movement of this century has failed to mobilize Christians for world evangelization. Furthermore, some of the superaggressive churches tend to act like minidenominations. Denominations will not go away. Those which refuse to be renewed, and who thus fail to be faithful stewards of the gospel, will be bypassed and will be relegated to the brackish backwaters of church growth.

There is nothing intrinsically evil about denominations. Denominations have given a strong forward thrust

OBSTACLES TO ITS FLOW

to world evangelization. The attitude that denominations are evil is itself an obstinate obstacle to church growth.

The unprintable signs.[11] These are not physical signs which we nail to our church doors. We don't print them and advertise them. Nevertheless, they are present for anyone to read who has eyes to see. The unprintable signs are really the body language of a congregation. One of those signs says: "The only people we expect here are those who have already been here." No one is posted to help strangers find their way around. No one is present to greet visitors. A stranger doesn't know whether he is headed toward the worship area or the kitchen.

A related sign says: "We have no competency in dealing with strangers here." It's OK if strangers will make themselves known to the members. The prevailing attitude toward visitors seems to be: "If they'll meet us halfway, we'll give them a lukewarm welcome." There is no genuine ritual of welcome in such congregations.

During the last seventeen years I have visited hundreds of churches. I have been indelibly impressed by the signs which are *not* displayed, and by the signs which are *unwittingly* displayed. Both the unprinted and the unprintable signs are real obstacles to church growth. They are much more important than some think.

Theological Obstacles

A second class of obstacles to church growth may be labeled theological. Sin is a theological obstacle. For example, the sin of showing partiality obstructs church growth. James focuses God's spotlight on the sin of partiality: "My brethren, show no partiality as you hold the faith of our Lord Jesus Christ, the Lord of glory. For if a man with gold rings and in fine clothing comes into your assembly, and a poor man in shabby clothing also comes in, and you pay attention to the one who wears the fine clothing and say, 'Have a seat here, please,' while you say to the poor man, 'Stand there,' or 'Sit at my feet,' have you not made distinctions among yourselves, and become judges with evil thoughts?'' (2:1-4).

Paul singles out the sin of divisions and strife over church leaders as an obstacle to church growth. The church at Corinth was split four ways. There were those who claimed to belong to Apollos, Cephas, Paul, and Christ. Paul questions them thusly: "Is Christ divided? Was Paul crucified for you? Or were you baptized in the name of Paul?" (1 Cor. 1:13). Paul's conclusion was: "What then is Apollos? What is Paul? Servants through whom you believed, as the Lord assigned to each. I planted, Apollos watered, but God gave the growth. So neither he who plants nor he who waters is anything, but only God who gives the growth. He who plants and he who waters are equal, and each shall receive his wages according to his labor. For we are God's fellow workers" (3:5-9).

A third example of the kind of sin which hinders church growth is the way the Corinthian church winked at immorality in their fellowship. The incident is mentioned in 1 Corinthians 5:1-2. "It is actually reported that there is immorality among you, and of a kind that is not found even among pagans; for a man is living with his father's wife. And you are arrogant! Ought you not rather to mourn? Let him who has done this be removed from among you."

A church which takes sin lightly and treats it flippantly is erecting a dam across the church growth river. Sin of every kind, whether personal or social, must be taken seriously if a church is to produce that fruit which pleases God. God is holy and just. He requires holiness and justice from his people.

Some Christians apparently think planning for growth is unspiritual. This is a second theological obstacle to the church growth river. Especially is it difficult for some Christians to see how long-range planning should have a role in the church. The return of Christ may appear to be so imminent to some that their eschatology actually prevents them from putting their hearts into planning for the future.

Part of this opposition to planning may arise from misunderstanding what planning entails. Edward Dayton tells us what planning is not: "Planning is not deciding in advance each step we are going to take and then faithfully following these predetermined steps. Planning is not trying to decide for God what He is going to do. Planning is not the imposition of one person's ideas upon another's."[12]

Rather, planning is more like an arrow which attempts to point the direction for a church. Dayton gathers up the essence of planning in these words:

> Planning is an attempt to write a history of the future—to us planning "under God." In one sense the "present" never exists; it is just the dividing line between what has happened in the past and what is yet to happen in the future. When we go through the process of planning, we try to think through the circumstances that lie ahead based upon the history that lies behind. We do this (1) so that we will encounter fewer surprises, (2) so that we can be effective stewards of the gift God has given us, and (3) so that we can measure our progress against objectives.[13]

Hence, if you are opposed to planning because you feel that it seeks to usurp the sovereignty of God, it need not and should not. I see nothing unspiritual with humanity seeking to shape the future. And for redeemed humanity to refuse to help shape the future is to be an unfaithful steward of God-given resources.

A third closely related theological obstacle to church growth is a lack of balance between the sovereignty of God and the freedom and responsibility of humanity. An overemphasis upon the sovereignty of God expresses itself in double-edged predestination on the one hand and in universalism on the other hand.

Double-edged predestination is the belief that certain persons are predestinated to salvation and that certain other persons are predestinated to damnation, and there isn't much that either group can do about it, or anything much we can or should do about it. Universalism doesn't take sin seriously enough. It is the belief that all will ultimately be saved regardless of their response to Christ in this life, and we shouldn't be too concerned about it. The old, original Hardshell Baptists exemplify the false doctrine of double-edged predestination, while the Unitarians and Universalists exemplify the false doctrine of Universalism.

Both double-edged predestination and Universalism are formidable obstacles to church growth. Unfortunately, these doctrines are not limited to the Hardshells and the Unitarians and Universalists. They have exponents and adherents in almost every denomination. I know of nothing which so cuts the heart out of evangelism and missions as these caricatures of God's sovereignty.

In addition to double-edged predestination and Universalism there is another caricature of God's sovereignty which hinders certain types of church growth. I refer to that brand of eschatology which focuses so exclusively upon the future that the present is almost blotted out. We can look so intently toward an apocalyptic solution to our problems that we fail to address ourselves responsibly to correcting the evils which abound. Incarnational growth has no place, or little place, on the agenda of those who look only to heaven for a solution to the ills of mankind.

It is interesting to note that Charles G. Finney, who was the last outstanding itinerant evangelist to be deeply concerned with what Costas calls incarnational church growth, was a postmillennialist. Finney saw "the reformation of mankind" as the "appropriate work" of the church. He wanted to see the churches as a body, and not just as individual Christians, involved in such moral reforms as the abolition of slavery, prohibition, and the eradication of prostitution.

We must recall that Finney, the flaming evangelist who led so many thousands of souls to Christ and into the churches, was president of Oberlin, the first coeducational college in the world. It was Finney who said: "The great business of the church is to reform the world—to put away every kind of sin. The church of Christ was originally organized to be a body of reformers."

Finney was not content with resolutions and "moral suasion." He wanted the churches to employ the government to secure legislation which would put the abominations away. Finney wrote in one of his letters on revivals: "It is melancholy and amazing to see to what an extent the church treats the different branches of reform either with indifference, or with direct opposition. There is not, I venture to say upon the whole earth an inconsistency more monstrous, more God-dishonoring and I must say more manifestly insane than the attitude which many of the churches take in respect to nearly every branch of reform which is needed among mankind."[14]

I am not advocating any millenial position. The only point I wish to make is that the church growth advocate must make an effort to hold in creative paradox both God's sovereignty and man's responsibility.

A fourth theological obstacle to church growth is paying lip service only to the priesthood of believers. Once western Europe was the center of gravity for the church. Today that center has shifted to North America. Some think the center might shift to Africa by the end of this century. But look at what has happened to the church in western Europe. Church attendance is down to 5 percent or less in places like France and England.

David Haney asked a seminary professor in Paris what happened to the church in western Europe. The professor answered: "The domination of the clergy!" Even though the Protestant Reformation championed the doctrine of the priesthood of the believer, the Protestant churches gradually moved toward a "priest mentality," whereby only the clergy were perceived to be priests.

Haney then asked the professor why the churches moved away from the priesthood of the believer. The professor answered: "The abdication of the laity."[15] We shall have to break out of that cycle if massive church growth is to be achieved.

McGavran wrote in 1965: "The traditional idea of the pastoral monopoly of evangelism should give way to the idea that every member should be an evangelist."[16] Melvin Hodges of the Assemblies of God spelled out seven obstacles to church growth in 1970. Among those was what Hodges called the "pastor-do-it-all" mentality.[17] The pastoral monopoly on evangelism must go. The pastor-do-it-all mentality must be jettisoned. Only then can the commas be erased from Ephesians 4:12. I propose that pastors take the initiative in breaking that growth inhibiting cycle to which the Paris professor pointed.

Kenneth Strachan of the Latin American Mission set forth the "Strachan theorem." The "Strachan theorem" says: "The successful expansion of any movement is in direct proportion to its success in mobilizing and occupying its total membership in constant propagation of its beliefs." Strachan, as George Peters reminds us, was wrong in concluding that, "this alone and nothing else is the key." Nevertheless, the theorem is important when held in tension with other essentials.[18]

We may have focused too exclusively upon men like Paul, Peter, Barnabas, and Silas in seeking to understand church growth in the first century. John Seamands calls our attention to some of the lay witnesses in the book of Acts:

> Stephen, a waiter on tables, who disputed with the Jews in the synagogue and became the first martyr of the Christian Church; Philip, another waiter, who became a leading lay-evangelist in the early Church; Lydia, a seller of cloth, who was a leading member of the church at Philippi; Aquila and Priscilla, tentmakers, who expounded the way of Christ more fully to an eloquent preacher of the Word; and Luke, missionary doctor, who gave us his biography of Christ and the history of the early Church. But we must add to this list a multitude of unnamed followers of Christ, who, when they were scattered abroad through persecution, went everywhere preaching the Word (Acts 8:1-4).[19]

Ecclesiastical Obstacles

Now, let us consider a third class of obstacles to church growth. Add to the attitudinal and theological obstacles a set of ecclesiastical obstacles.

Short pastorates are certainly one ecclesiastical obstacle. Lyle Schaller has said: "Long pastorates do not automatically produce growing churches, but there are no growing churches who change pastors every two or three years."[20] A church with a passing parade of pastors can just about write church growth off of its agenda. And a pastor or other full-time staff members who move every two or three years need not be bothered too much with church growth pains.

Church growth which is lasting requires top, incarnational leadership. Persons will not readily follow a leader who has no permanent investment in what happens to them and to their church. They need a stable pastor who lives among them and who can truly identify with their plight and problems. The nonresidential pastor seldom leads a church to grow. That may be one reason church growth is so lacking in many churches of America. Their pastors so often don't live among the people.

Another closely related obstacle is the leadership style of the pastor. The shepherd model is traditional with pastors and churches. That model works fine, says Schaller, as long as a congregation doesn't grow to beyond seventy or eighty families. When you go beyond that number, a rancher model becomes necessary. Look at the typical Episcopal church for example. In an Episcopal parish the bishop is the rancher. He depends upon the foreman and others to do some things.

New missions require a shepherd. But as congregations grow the shepherd must change his style to that of a rancher. That change in roles creates confusion which blocks growth. If, however, the pastor of a growing church cannot delegate to others some of his shepherding functions, he will either impede growth or will have to move on to another field. The congregation will also have to make the shift in role expectations. If not, they will either impede growth or "kill" their pastor.

This may be an appropriate place to mention understaffing as an obstacle to church growth. Some churches are staffed for decline, some for stability, and some for growth. Very few are staffed for growth. Schaller, as a rule of thumb, thinks if a church is running 200 in worship attendance, it needs one staff member; if 300 it needs two; if 400 it needs three; and if 500 it needs four. The older a congregation is, the more staff members it needs.

If you run 300 in worship attendance on Sunday morning and have only a pastor and a secretary, you are probably staffed for decline. If you run 300 in worship, have a pastor and one other full-time program person with two secretaries, you are probably staffed for stability. Now, if such a church would add one full- or part-time program person to that staff, it would be staffed for growth.[21]

Occasionally congregations get cold feet. They begin to cut back on staff, to merge classes, to cut out services, and so forth. This "cut-back" syndrome is a real obstacle to church growth. It even infects entire denominations at times. Especially is this evident in the way some denominations have cut back on their foreign missionaries and their national staffs.

Congregations start cutting back for a variety of reasons. Some cut out services so as to save energy. After all, there is an energy crisis. Others feel that they can get to know persons better if they all worship at one time and in the same place. It is of course easier to know and to be known, the smaller the group.

The trouble with that kind of reasoning, Schaller points out, is that mergers of 4 + 4 do not always equal 8. If you merge two classes of ten members each, that does not equal twenty. If you merge two worship services of 200 in one and 100 in the other, that does not equal 300 in attendance at the one combined service. Yet, we frequently fall victims to such fallacious logic.

Denominational Xeroxing in programs and methods can become a formidable ecclesiastical obstacle to church growth. Church growth must not degenerate into denominational franchising. Local creativity and innovation cease only at the peril of falling victim to brand-name Christianity. The local church which feels disloyal to the denomination because it tries something different or new in its programs or methods has fallen victim to denominational Xeroxing.

Fortunately, most denominations now offer their churches a smorgasbord of programs and materials. They encourage rather than stifle creativity. Their best programs are first tried and proven in the laboratory of some local church or churches.

From time to time churches also become prisoners of their own institutionalism. They get trapped by a building indebtedness, or find themselves custodians of property which they cannot afford. Some pastors have led churches to erect monuments to their own egos, to over-build. This is one of those obstacles to church growth which might have been prevented through sound planning and more faithful stewardship.

Finally, a whole string of obstacles fall under the heading of ecclesiastical pathology, or church diseases. Peter Wagner has become an expert on ecclesiastical diseases. Wagner diagnoses eight diseases, two of which he says are fatal. The other six may be overcome.[22]

Ethnikitis is one of the eight. It is terminal and has to do with the changing church in a changing neighborhood. "Where the church is virtually an island of one kind of people in the midst of a community of another, with very little communication between the two, you have ethnikitis."

Ethnikitis is failure to understand and apply the homogenous unit principle in church planning. From 1966 to 1973, seven Southern Baptist churches in Birmingham, Alabama died from ethnikitis. "Three died in four years, and none lasted more than eight years after ethnikitis set in."

Another example is the Trinity Baptist Church of Kansas City. In 1973 Trinity had a terrible case of ethnikitis. Its neighborhood experienced white flight and an influx of blacks. Trinity donated its $175,000 building to Spruce St. Matthews Baptist Church, a struggling black congregation. Two years later Spruce St. Matthews had grown from 100 to 500 in attendance.[23]

Old age is another of the eight. It, too, is terminal. Like those afflicted with ethnikitis, these churches cannot do much growing because they are dying. But unlike ethnikitis, old age tends to occur in rural areas rather than urban. The disease is caused by demographic shifts. Children are not available for biological growth, and it is impossible to bring in young blood from surrounding communities. Following a period of pastoral care, churches afflicted with old age die.

People blindness is a recoverable disease, and another of Wagner's eight. Some call this "Sociopsychological Tissue Rejection." People blindness is the failure to see the differences between E-1 evangelism and E-2 and E-3 evangelism. E-1 evangelism is among our own kind of people, whereas E-2 and E-3 are evangelism among people of a different culture. Those who have "people vision" can see the subgroups within a country which are significant to a strategy for evangelism. Those who are afflicted with people blindness tend to see all Americans as Americans. However, those who have people vision can see that not only are there major differences among Americans, but there are even significant differences among Anglos and blacks and Hispanics and Asians, and so forth.

New churches are needed for people won through E-2 and E-3 evangelism. New methods may be needed to do E-2 and E-3 evangelism than those which prove successful for E-1 evangelism. Otherwise the different subgroups will tend to reject the new tissue. Some churches are not growing because they have people blindness.

Hypercooperativism is a fourth of these diseases. "It is based," says Wagner, "on the false premise that the more churches of different denominations cooperate with each other, the better they will collectively evangelize." Key 73 was an example of hypercooperativism. Here is a disease which affects the Evangelicals as well as the ecumenists.

Contrary to the premise on which hypercooperativism is built, says Wanger, "the opposite is more likely true. Chances are the more that churches cooperate interdenominationally in evangelistic programs, the less effective the effort turns out in the end." Apparently evangelism which actually produces church growth begins and ends with a local church.

Koinonitis is a fifth church growth disease identified by Wagner. This is fellowship inflamation, or too much of a good thing. "Churches which have discovered that they have a wide open back door and that tend to lose members as fast as they gain them would do well to examine their fellowship groups for koinonitis." This is the obstacle which Hodges calls a "family-clan mentality."[24]

There is no room for newcomers in koinonitis. Such churches tend to turn inward and away from evangelism. While koinonitis is not inherent in lay renewal, the charismatic movement, and the Keswick movement, these movements are especially susceptible to the disease. Insofar as such movements create a spiritual elite in the churches, and broaden "the sanctification gap," they become carriers of koinonitis.

A sixth of these diseases is sociological strangulation. This disease occurs "when the people flow in a church moves beyond the capacity of the facilities to handle it." Garden Grove Community Church was afflicted with sociological strangulation in 1979. The congregation plans to overcome the disease by building a new sanctuary which will double its present capacity of 2,000.

Arrested spiritual development is another disease. This is the lack of internal growth. The congregation remains babes in Christ. They are starving for the Word of God, and not growing outwardly because they are not growing inwardly and spiritually. They may have inverted their priorities.

St. John's syndrome is the eighth disease which Wagner discusses. Named after St. John who first wrote of the disease, this is the church which like Ephesus has left its first love (Rev. 2:4). Wagner thinks the first love of Ephesus was evangelism. The church at Ephesus had become affluent. She suffered from what church growth terminology calls "redemption and lift." The entire passage of Revelation 2:1-7 should be studied to get the full meaning of St. John's syndrome. Churches do fall into sick syndromes. Apart from repentance and the surgery of the Great Physician, a church cannot break out of St. John's syndrome.

Two other church growth diseases which I have heard mentioned are Laodicean lethargy and acute doctrinitis. Laodicean lethargy is lukewarmness, a temperature too low to please God. Acute doctrinitis is doctrine inflamation where Christians get to loving doctrine more than they love God and the Fourth World.

11. Its Contributions to Evangelism

Every river makes contributions to those who use its waters. What are some of the contributions which the church growth river makes to evangelism? Tom Huston, executive director of the British and Foreign Bible Society, expressed it this way: "The Great Commission has had a face lift in the 1970s. Instead of being spoken of mostly in terms of evangelism, the emphasis has begun to shift to church growth. This is a development which will, more than anything else, control the progress of Christianity in the 1980s."[1]

Church growth has made, and is making, a number of contributions to evangelism. One of its contributions is a new definition of evangelism: "to proclaim Jesus Christ as God and Savior, to persuade people to become his disciples and responsible members of his church."[2] Note the high Christology in that definition, "Jesus Christ as God and Savior." Further, note the twin emphasis on "proclaim" and "persuade." Church growth leaders make much of the three "p's" in evangelism: presence, proclamation, and persuasion. Then, note the emphasis on "disciples" rather than decisions. Church growth is concerned with Great Commission missions and evangelism, such as is found in Matthew 28:18-20. Finally, note the emphasis in the definition on "responsible" church membership.

An emphasis upon the cultural element in evangelism is a second contribution made by church growth. Church growth exhibits an awareness of the cultural distance between the evangelist and the person to be evangelized. That distance is expressed through the symbols E-0, E-1, E-2, and E-3. E-0 evangelism is evangelizing lost church members. It crosses no cultural barriers. E-1 evangelism is evangelizing one's own kind, but it crosses the stained-glass barrier and moves out to persons who are outsiders to the family of God. E-2 evangelism is evangelizing persons who belong to another cultural group. Perhaps they represent pockets of subcultures within our own community, such as persons who speak a language other than English as their mother tongue. E-2 evangelism crosses both the stained-glass barrier and at least one cultural barrier. E-3 evangelism is evangelizing persons who are foreigners to us. It is what we call foreign missions.[3]

Church growth leaders are certain that evangelism never occurs in a cultural vacuum, but always in a particular cultural context. They know that the evangelist should exhibit an awareness of his own culture, the culture of the persons whom he seeks to evangelize, and the culture out of which the biblical message arises.[4]

The Willowbank Report on Gospel and Culture defined culture as follows: "Culture is an integrated system of beliefs (about God or reality, or ultimate meaning), of values (how to behave, relate to others, talk, pray, dress, work, play, trade, farm, eat, etc.), and of institutions which express these beliefs, values and customs (government, law courts, temples or churches, family, schools, hospitals, factories, shops, unions, clubs, etc.), which bind a society together and gives it a sense of identity, dignity, security, and community."[5]

This cultural awareness of church growth permits (and even commends) the use of anthropology, psychology, marketing research, communications theory, and computer technology in the service of evangelism.

It also accounts for the controversial, homogeneous unit principle in church growth. Professor McGavran

125

defines a HU as "a section of society in which all members have some characteristic in common."[6] He also makes the well-known statement that persons "like to become Christians without crossing racial, linguistic or class barriers."[7]

America is not a melting pot; it is a stewing pot. More than 43 percent of all Americans are unmelted, and may be unmeltable.[8] The HU principle offers us a realistic beginning point in evangelizing this mosaic of peoples.[9]

Church growth focuses on the corporate as well as the individual in evangelism. McGavran makes much of the conversion of whole families in the New Testament. His early writings spoke of people movements and group conversion. Now, a new phrase has been created to describe the corporate nature of conversion. That phrase is "multiindividual mutually-interdependent decision."[10] Perhaps the best analogy to explain what the phrase means is that of marriage. When two persons decide to get married, their's is a multiindividual mutually-interdependent decision. Church growth leaders are concerned with spiritual multiplication, and not just spiritual addition, in evangelism. They want to see the structures of family, tribe, caste, and other *ta ethne,* converted to Jesus Christ. They do not believe the world can be evangelized in one generation by picking converts off one by one, or by near neighbor evangelism, or by the traditional institutional approach of the mission station and the mission compound.[11]

This corporate element in evangelism should make us more conscious of the role of the family in evangelism. If it is good to convert one member of a family to Christ, it is even better to convert two or more members of that family to Christ. A lone Christian in a family has no support from those nearest and dearest to him or her. The family is a social-economic structure which needs to be converted to Jesus Christ.

Michael Green and Tom Wolf call this *"oikos* evangelism."[12] Church growth is committed to *oikos* evangelism, to household evangelism.

A fourth contribution of church growth to evangelism is closely allied to the corporate element. We are made keenly aware that the natural and normal networks of kinship, friendship, and association are the bridges across which God moves into the lives of persons. We might call this "web evangelism." Christians are to use their web of kin and friends to get the gospel to the world.[13]

Win Arn found that in the Billy Graham Seattle Crusade 83 percent of those who made decisions, and were one year later incorporated into churches, had friends or relatives already in those churches.[14]

Another aspect of web evangelism is that the new convert is probably in touch with more lost prospects when he or she confesses faith in Christ than he or she will ever be. Generally speaking, the longer one is a Christian, the fewer lost persons one knows. While James Eaves was pastoring First Baptist Church, Albuquerque, New Mexico, a cocktail waitress was converted. She invited all of her loved ones and friends to attend her baptismal service. She threw a party for them at her home following her baptismal service. Dr. Eaves was invited to the party and was requested to share a few words. At least seventeen of that lady's kinfolk and friends were eventually converted to Christ.[15]

When the Gerasene demoniac was converted, he begged Jesus that he might go with him. Jesus refused, and said: "Go home to your friends, and tell them how much the Lord has done for you" (Mark. 5:19). I am coming to feel that the most logical person to win my lost friends and family members to Christ is I.

Church growth thinking destroys the old myth that we are too close to our own family and friends to lead them to Christ. As a matter of fact, we may be the very bridges across which God will move into their lives.

The pyramid principle is a fifth contribution of church growth to evangelism. This principle says that "for a church to grow it must expand its base of organization and ministry before it may add to its mass of followers."[16] If you want to build a larger pyramid, you have to enlarge its base.

Some evangelism has so concentrated on adding numbers to the body that the structure which holds that body has been overwhelmed. We saw this especially in some early models of bus evangelism.

One church of my acquaintance operated a large fleet of buses. Several hundred persons were bused in each Sunday—especially children. All of the adults were removed from their classrooms and merged into one big pastor's class which met in the auditorium. The stated rationale for this was that the space was needed more for the children. I was not surprised to hear that the Achilles' heel of that congregation was its finances. That church was violating the pyramid principle. It was adding to its mass of followers without enlarging its base of organization and ministry.

The church which in its evangelistic zeal keeps adding to its followers without a corresponding expansion of its organizational and leadership base is like Humpty Dumpty who sat on a wall. It will fall, and no one can put it together again. That's what happened to the church which merged all of its adults into one huge pastor's class to make way for a twentieth-century children's crusade!

A renewed emphasis upon spiritual gifts is a sixth contribution of church growth to evangelism. This comes to us via Pentecostalism and neo-Pentecostalism. Peter Wagner is the most articulate spokesman for the use of spiritual gifts in evangelism. Wagner's book on the subject is entitled *Your Spiritual Gifts Can Help Your Church*

Grow.[17] He contends that while every Christian is a witness, only about 10 percent of any congregation will have the gift of an evangelist. The only exception Wagner has found to that is the Coral Ridge Presbyterian Church in Fort Lauderdale, Florida.[18]

All of the gifts are for body building (i.e., building up the church which is the body of Christ). "If everybody in the church is expected to be an evangelist," asks Wagner, "where are those with all the other spiritual gifts that are needed to make those with the gift of an evangelist more effective?"[19]

Wagner suggests five steps for discovering one's spiritual gift: (1) Explore the possibilities; (2) Experiment with as many as possible; (3) Examine your feelings; (4) Evaluate your effectiveness; (5) Expect confirmation from the body.[20]

This emphasis on spiritual gifts does at least three things for evangelism. First, it emphasizes that evangelism is spiritual work which requires spiritual persons who have spiritual power. It lifts up the role of the Holy Spirit in evangelism. Second, it points to the liberation of the laity. The gifts are bestowed on all of God's people. Third, it helps build a healthy ego in the rank and file members of the body. Each Christian is a gifted member.

The use of a medical model in evangelism is a seventh contribution. Church growth leaders speak of "body evangelism." They use phrases such as "church growth eyes" and "discerning the body." Dr. Merton Alexander, a medical doctor, is credited by Dr. McGavran for the latter two phrases. Peter Wagner credits Vergil Gerber for the term "body evangelism" although I cannot find the term in Gerber's *God's Way to Keep a Church Going and Growing.*[21]

This medical model permits us to examine the evangelistic health of the church. How can we tell whether a church is healthy or sick in its evangelism? We can use the discipling test, the equipping test, the symmetrical test, the leadership test, and the missionary test. Such tests address themselves to certain questions: Are we adding new disciples to the body of Christ? Are we equipping the church members to intentionally share their faith? Does our evangelism exhibit symmetry in its methodology and its theology? Are the pastor, the church staff, the church council, the deacons, and the other church officers committed to evangelism? Is this church concerned with extension and bridging growth as well as with expansion growth?[22]

Peter Wagner appropriates this medical model to speak of the pathology of church growth. He identifies eight church diseases as follows: ethnikitis, old age, people-blindness, hypercooperativism, koinonitis, sociological strangulation, arrested spiritual development, and St. John's syndrome.[23]

A positive attitude toward numerical growth in evangelism is an eighth contribution of church growth. Church growth spokesmen believe that we are living in the sunrise rather than in the sunset of evangelism. They see numbers as shorthand for persons. They ask why we should count budgets and buildings and books, and not count persons?

Church growth leaders destroy the myth that the golden age of evangelism is in the past. They convince us that the golden age for evangelism is in the present, and in the future. McGavran says: "There are more winnable people in the world today than ever before."[24] McGavran continues: "The Christian Church stands *at the beginning of her mission.* The minor church growth of the nineteenth and twentieth centuries is only the prologue. The great turnings to Christ and the mighty multiplications of His churches lie ahead. The era of church plantings has only just begun."[25]

Realistic, measurable, faith goals are established and monitored in evangelism by church growth consultants. MBO (Management by Objectives) is welcomed by them. "Planning is most effective," said Edward R. Dayton, "when the entire Christian enterprise is led by men who are committed to managing by objectives."[26] McGavran even contends that every mission board should devote 5 percent of its budget to research.[27]

Wagner goes so far as to spell out rates of growth which might be incorporated into a congregation's evangelistic goals. A 25 percent per decade growth rate is *poor.* That is no more than biological growth, merely reaching the children of church members. A 50 percent per decade growth rate is *fair* in the USA and Canada. A 100 percent per decade growth rate is *good.* That means you are doing something right. A 200 percent per decade growth rate is *excellent;* 300 percent is *outstanding;* and 500 percent is *incredible.*[28] Yet, Garden Grove Community Church in Orange County, California grew at a rate in excess of 500 percent per decade for over eighteen years. When you reach a 200 percent decadal growth rate, you can start conducting conferences on how you do it, and persons will attend in large numbers.

Church growth leaders advocate discarding worn-out and nonproductive methods in evangelism. Evangelistic methods are never sacred to church growth. This is a tenth contribution of church growth.

Win Arn has forthrightly questioned the Billy Graham method of crusade evangelism,[29] and the "Here's Life America" mass media blitz of Campus Crusade.[30] The most devastating critique of Crusade's "I Found It" campaign was done by Peter Wagner in *Eternity* magazine.[31] Church growth is ruthless and pragmatic in evaluating evangelistic methods. No evangelistic method is "Off Limits" to church growth practitioners.

Perhaps the best known example where church growth has discarded a worn-out, unproductive method of evangelism is its advocacy of the new messianic synagogue model versus the old Hebrew Christian model. Phillip E. Goble, who wrote the book *Everything You Need to Grow a Messianic Synagogue,* perfected his model while he was studying at Fuller Seminary.[32]

Church growth also provides some tools for testing balance in our evangelism. McGavran, for example, posits five classes of church leaders.[33] Class 1 are volunteer leaders reaching inward. Class 2 are volunteer leaders reaching outward. Class 3 are bivocational leaders who are partially paid for their church work. Class 4 are full-time paid leaders such as pastors and other church staff personnel. Class 5 are denominational leaders whose ministry is cast with no one local church. The typical church which compares its five classes of leaders will find a terrible imbalance between class 2 and class 1 leaders. One reason many churches are not growing is that they have so few class 2 leaders.

McGavran and his colleagues contend that churches grow numerically through *biological, transfer,* or *conversion* growth.[34] An analysis of many churches will reveal that the conversion growth is out of balance with biological and transfer growth.

Still a third tool for testing balance is to compare the types of growth in a church. McGavran and his colleagues teach four types of growth: internal, expansion, extension, and bridging.[35] Orlando Costas teaches four types of growth somewhat different: numerical, organic, conceptual, and incarnational.[36] Belew calls bridging growth "sending growth," and incarnational growth "prophetic growth," or the "voice to the world" growth, by which he means taking a stance on social issues.[37]

Whichever terminology you prefer, test the evangelistic balance of your congregation by the several types of growth. Some churches are concerned almost only with internal growth. Others are consumed only with expansion growth. Some are total strangers to incarnational growth, and so forth.

12. Its Possible Pollution

Every river is subject to pollution. That pollution tends to flow through the whole stream and to permeate the whole river, although it may be worse in certain places along the river's course than in others. To illustrate, not too long ago I saw persons swimming and playing in the Mississippi River near Elk River, Minnesota. But, I have never seen anyone swimming in the Mississippi as it flows through St. Louis, Missouri.

The church growth river is not much different from all other rivers in respect to pollution. Church growth is indeed subject to pollution and should not be assumed to be crystal clear and pure like sweet spring water. Let us examine its possible biblical, theological, and adiaphorous pollution.

Biblical Pollution

Erroneous Interpretation. The church growth movement occasionally interprets the Bible erroneously so as to support preconceived points of view. A most glaring example is McGavran's erroneous interpretation of Matthew 28:19-20 to support his presupposition that discipling and perfecting can be separated. Accurate exegesis of the passage does not support, and in fact contradicts, McGavran's forced interpretation.

The phrases about baptizing and teaching are not temporal, sequential acts to the phrase about discipling the nations. Rather, they are concomitant phrases which indicate two ways of carrying out the imperative command to make disciples. One way to make disciples is to baptize them into the name of the holy Trinity. Another way to make disciples is by teaching them to observe the commandments of Christ.

A second example of erroneous interpretation is Peter Wagner's use of the New Testament to support the homogeneous unit principle. Wagner says, "If this homogeneous unit principle is not the way New Testament churches developed, that's sufficient evidence to scrap it." Then, Wagner cites the twelve apostles as an example of the HU principle. Even so, he admits that Judas Iscariot was an exception. All the others, Wagner thinks, were Aramaic-speaking Galilean Jews. Wagner sees Matthias being chosen over Joseph Barsabbas to replace Judas because he too was an Aramaic-speaking Galilean Jew. Wagner insists that "Jesus started no Gentile church." "When the Syrophonecian woman came along," says Wagner, "Jesus used language that could be considered racist."[1]

All of this overlooks the exception of Judas Iscariot to the HU principle; ignores that there is no reference whatever in the text to the fact that Matthias was chosen because he *may* have been an Aramaic-speaking Galilean Jew; glosses over the possibility that Jesus' dealings with non-Jews may have been "deliberate teaching methods of his to break down the limited cultural background of the disciples"; and, does not acknowledge other possible nonracist interpretations of Jesus' words to the Syrophoenician woman. No wonder Ray Stedman can comment on Wagner's use of such Scriptures: "That's a beautiful example . . . of approaching Scriptures with a conclusion already in mind."[2]

McGavran does almost the same thing as Wagner with his discussion of people movements. He says Roland Allen "did not see the people movement at all." According to McGavran, "Allen missed the fact that Paul went to the great cities only because the Jews lived there."

McGavran thinks for the first twenty years there was no Gentile church. He accounts for that by his concept of people movements.[3]

Indeed, Wagner cites Acts 9:35 as specific New Testament examples of people movements.[4] Yet, another real possibility for the slowness in developing a Gentile church was the denseness and disobedience of the early disciples. Also, Acts 9:35 could be hyperbole, or might be taken as a kind of summary statement. DuBose is surely correct when he says: "The book of Acts recognizes this different cultural reality, but it does not cater to it."[5]

Biblical Criticism. The church growth movement neither models nor recommends a critical[6] approach to the use of the Bible. I find it ironical that a movement which wishes to be known as a new science would tout the critical study of sociology, psychology, anthropology, statistics, and so forth, but is so manifestly uncritical in its use of the Bible. Where is the call for a comparable use of biblical linguistics, archaeology, and the science of hermeneutics?

Great lip service is paid to the inspiration and authority of the Bible. But when some of the advocates of church growth use it, it becomes a book of proof texts with little awareness of the progressive nature of its revelation of God. I do not see enough use of Scripture among church growth advocates, nor do I see enough attention to undergirding church growth with the critical biblical study which it deserves and requires.

McGavran made a definitive statement on the Bible in 1974. He proposed that we take a high view of Scripture as a solution to "the uproar about cultures and Christianity." He affirmed verbal inspiration saying: "God used a current language and a current culture, but was not bound or limited by them. The writers, while immersed in their cultures, were *inspired and therefore not culture bound.*"[7]

McGavran equates the high view of Scripture with "propositional truth," concluding that those who have a low view of Scripture might tend to substitute "the infallibility of cultures for the infallibility of the Bible." Later, he says: "The Bible is part of the supracultural as well as part of the cultural."[8]

I share McGavran's high view of Scripture. Nevertheless, I confess I fail to comprehend how he can argue that the writers of the Bible were "not culture bound" if the Bible is indeed a part of the cultural as well as the supracultural. Moreover, I have trouble computing how McGavran can reconcile his view that the clash between Christianity and cultures "is confined to one or two percent"[9] and still contend that it is those who hold a low view of Scripture who tend to substitute the infallibility of cultures for the infallibility of the Bible. McGavran has about the highest view of cultures of any man I have read! He certainly fails to demonstrate that a low view of cultures results from a high view of the Scriptures.

It is possible that McGavran's high view of Scripture blinds him to the importance of critical Bible study. He seems to forget that the believer who holds such a high view of Scripture is himself or herself a creature of a culture, and that the interpreter will inevitably bring his or her cultural baggage and mind-set to the interpreter's house. When we cease to be culture-bound, we lose touch with our context.

So long as church growth exhibits this shallow hermeneutic, it will not gain the respect of those Christians who insist that we love God with our minds as well as with our other faculties. If church growth cannot withstand the searchlight of critical biblical studies, it will not capture the imagination of many potential allies.

Biblical Balance. A third possible source of biblical pollution in the church growth river is the lack of balance in church growth theology. McGavran's four types (internal, expansion, extension, and bridging) do not cover all of the biblical possibilities.

One of the points on which church growth should be graded poorly is its balance. Most objective readers of the church growth literature will admit that far more is said about expansion growth than any other kind. It is ironical that while Costas *numerical* growth as one of his four types, McGavran and his followers have far more to say about that type of growth than any other type. Moreover, when McGavran and his followers speak of expansion growth, they use the term synonomously with numerical growth.

My guess is that expansion (equals numerical) growth is so prominent in the literature because it has been so neglected by so many churches. Nevertheless, one could wish for much greater balance in the treatment of growth types.

One of the really strong points which recommends the book by Chaney and Lewis is their wholesome emphasis on extension growth. Yet, Chaney and Lewis no more treat internal and bridging growth than do most other books on church growth designed for American consumption. In their Preface they say: "This book is about *numerical* growth."[10]

Moreover, what Costas labels organic, conceptual, and incarnational types of church growth are almost totally lacking in the literature. Alan R. Tippett's *Church Growth and the Word of God* may be a noteworthy exception.[11]

Theological Pollution

The church growth movement has not been blessed with scholars who excel in biblical and theological studies. The biblical and theological undergirdings for the movement have not been adequately stated. Some of them have been put in place after the movement was on the way. Peter Wagner has boasted that the faculty members at Fuller Seminary's School of World Mission have earned their doctorates in areas such as anthropology, psychology, education, and history.[12] While I salute these men for enlisting those areas of knowledge in the service of church growth, I should like to hear what some of the church's biblical scholars and theologians have to say about church growth. Surely Arthur Glasser cannot be right in saying: "Nothing is more important but that the church grow."[13]

Change. There is little or no recognition of doctrinal change among church growth advocates. This is strange because they make so much of the role of change in shaping receptivity to the gospel. Doctrine to the church growth school tends to be a set of divinely given propositional truths. They appear to be contented with the doctrines which have been handed down to us especially through Calvin and the other reformers. Yet, every Christian doctrine has a particular history. One of the most clearly demonstrable things about doctrine is that it is always evolving and changing, shaping and being reshaped as it is applied to different cultures and in different periods of history.

You read the church growth literature in vain searching for any serious dialogue with the contemporary ferment in theology. If contemporary approaches to theology are treated, they are rejected forthrightly in favor of such documents as the Frankfurt Declaration.[14]

The Bible itself reveals to us a God whose name is "I AM WHO I AM" [or "I WILL BE WHAT I WILL BE"] (Ex. 3:14). Our God is one who changes his mind in response to our prayers. He is a loving Father who is sensitive to the needs and petitions of his children.

I think this insensitivity to the role of change in doctrine may account for the displeasure toward dialogue in the evangelism model advocated by some church growth advocates. An adequate theory of communications requires feedback. Moreover, the communication of the gospel must be done totally and not just verbally. If evangelism is a matter of proclamation only, then we can load our gospel truck up with a set of propositional truths and drive all over the world dumping them on people. It doesn't cost as much to practice "dump truck" evangelism.

Pragmatism. The church growth movement so elevates pragmatism in theology that it perpetuates what Timothy Smith has termed "the Great Reversal."[15] I shall call it the Great Divide. The Great Divide which some Christians want to make between evangelism and ethics, between a personal gospel and a social gospel, between tell-evangelism and do-evangelism, and so forth, is personified in McGavran and Wagner.

McGavran and Wagner insist that the Great Commission must take priority over the great commandment. I strongly disagree, and along with David Moberg call for "a reversal of the Great Reversal." Moberg is right: "We are not required to select between this-worldliness and otherworldliness, for salvation relates to both."[16]

McGavran and Wagner want us to ask the pragmatic question prior to the ethical question. The pragmatic question asks, "Will it work?" The ethical question asks, "Is it right?" McGavran and Wagner play down the social implications of the gospel. This is done not so much by pitting evangelism against social action as by giving top priority to changing the person rather than his or her society. Peter Wagner is certain that churches should give *no* priority to social action. Wagner's opinion is: "If churches are to develop a social ministry (and I think they should), they will do well if they stick to social service and leave social action to other organizations, both secular and Christian."[17] Hence, it is all right for churches to be good Samaritans. However, it is all wrong for them to correct the conditions which caused the man to be robbed and beaten and left for dead! Church growth proponents seem to forget that the same one who gave the Great Commission also gave the twin love commandments.

There are three problems with believing that changed persons will change society. First, all persons will never be changed. Second, even every converted person is never completely converted in this life. There are always unconverted areas in one's life. Perfection awaits another world. Third, too many persons who claim to have been changed by God do little or nothing to change society.

This pragmatism also accounts for prophecy being a missing or muted element in church growth. By prophecy I mean forthtelling the Word of God. Church growth people tend to introduce a dichotomy between the New Testament evangelist and the Old Testament prophet. They seem to want to avoid the "prophetic tension" which the church should bring to bear upon the world.

Wilfred Bockleman tells about a visit to Garden Grove Community Church. He asked one of the staff members how the church fulfilled its prophetic function. The staff member quickly replied: "We are a nonprophetic church." Thinking that the staff member may have misunderstood the meaning of his word *prophetic,* Bockleman explained that he meant, "How does the church address the social issues of the day?" Again the staff member replied: "We are a nonprophetic church. Our people witness on the job by telling others about Christ and the church and by helping heal the hurts of society and by tithing."[18]

The community of faith should be involved in the life

and problems of its social environment. It should participate in the afflictions of its world. It should be a spokesperson for the weak and destitute. Jesus, the model church growth person, announced his mission with a prophetic text:

"The Spirit of the Lord is upon me,
because he has anointed me to preach good news to the
    poor.
He has sent me to proclaim release to the captives and
    recovering of sight to the blind,
to set at liberty those who are oppressed,
to proclaim the acceptable year of the Lord"
    (Luke 4:18-19).

Accommodation. The church growth movement may have been polluted also by theological accommodation. Its terminology has been accommodated to fit conservative evangelicals. For example, McGavran started out talking about people movements and group conversion. He has found it expedient to accommodate that terminology to the more palatable phrase: "multiindividual mutually interdependent decision."[19]

A second and far-reaching aspect of this accommodation is the almost sacred role which McGavran and his colleagues give to mission societies in world evangelization. They cannot conceive of world evangelization apart from voluntary mission societies. Yoder points out that McGavran's movement has found a clientele in the EFMA (Evangelical Foreign Missions Association), the IFMA (Interdenominational Foreign Mission Association) and the NAE (National Association of Evangelicals) related churches.[20]

Voluntary mission societies come close to being the *one* sacred method for the church growth school. I am suggesting that both of these accommodations fit the theological clientele of conservative evangelicals who have warmly welcomed McGavran and his colleagues.

Our terminology, methodology, and our theology are shaped to some extent by the company we keep. Our theological friends and family do have a bearing on the way we talk and act.

Reductionism. I see several kinds of theological reductionism in the church growth river—especially in its fountainhead. First, the locus of theology is reduced to ecclesiology. "The problem with a church-centered theology," says Costas, "is that it militates against the 'locus' of biblical theology: Christ."[21]

Note that theology tends to be reduced to ecclesiology in church growth. Its locus is not the kingdom of God or Christology, either of which would be more biblical than ecclesiology. The church is not synonomous with the kingdom of God. The kingdom of God is the pearl of great price, not the church.

Second, church growth blurs the line of demarcation between the church and the world, between Christ and culture. Can it be true that the clash between Christianity and cultures is "confined to one or two percent of the components"?[22] Can McGavran's three meanings of discipleship (D1, D2, and D3) be supported on theological grounds? Are D1, and possibly D2, discipleship incompatible with a believer's church?[23] Are persons indeed discipled when they "feel united around Jesus Christ as Lord and Saviour, believe themselves to be members of His Church, and realize that 'our folk are Christians, our book is the Bible, and our house is the church' "?[24]

Third, the church growth movement has no strongly developed corporate sense of sin and evil. The demonic elements in culture are treated too lightly by church growth advocates. This is all the more surprising because of the corporate sense of salvation in church growth. Sin to church growth theorists is primarily a matter of being out of fellowship with God.

Church growth majors on the one vertical relation

between God and men. The need for reconciliation between a person and his or her neighbor is a secondary and horizontal relation which must never usurp the priority of the vertical relation. Moreover, there is no recognition whatever to the importance of reconciliation between a person and the world of nature, or to the reconciliation of the self to his or her other self. Hence, there is a reductionism of these four, living, dialogical relations to the one vertical relation of persons to God.

I do not see a keen awareness in church growth of what Paul said in Ephesians 6:12: "For we are not contending against flesh and blood, but against the principalities, . . . against the world rulers of this present darkness, against the spiritual hosts of wickedness in the heavenly places."

Fourth, there is a subtle and unconscious attempt in church growth to reduce Christianity to a religion rather than a way of life. "Church growth theory," writes Ramseyer, "assumes that there is a general class of phenomena which can be designated 'religion' of which the Christian faith is one expression." If that is true, then, conversion becomes not so much "a resynthesis of one's basic orientation to self and the world, but rather the adoption of some new patterns in one limited aspect of that orientation."[25]

Adiaphorous Pollution

Finally, there is that class of pollution which may be called adiaphorous, or indifferent, because it is neither good or bad. Rather, it is mixed or neutral pollution. I shall mention four kinds of adiaphorous pollution.

Functionalism. A possible problem with church growth is its simplistic, functional approach toward such a complex phenomenon. One of my students did a paper in which he compared various steps, principles, signs, elements, commonalities, traits, characteristics, building blocks, and specifications for growing churches. He concluded by boiling it all down to five areas of agreement.[26] Hence, Peter Wagner writes about "Seven Vital Signs of a Healthy Church" in *Your Church Can Grow.*[27] McGavran and Arn title their 1977 book, *Ten Steps for Church Growth.*[28]

Dr. McGavran's opening remarks to the Academy for Evangelism in Theological Education in 1978 were something like this: "I hope each of you will discover your own principle of church growth and share it with the whole church." There were about forty or more persons in the room. Later in the dialogue with Professor McGavran, I inquired about the meaning of his opening remarks and asked him how many principles of church growth he thought there were. He replied that he was quite serious and that the principles were almost infinite in number![29] That kind of open-endedness coupled with simplistic, functional models bothers me.

Fantasying. There is some evidence that church growth advocates tend to live in a fantasy world. They tend to fantasize about superchurches and pastors. There is a subtle tendency to uncritically exalt superchurches above other churches. Peter Wagner does this in his discussion of worship.[30] Big is not necessarily beautiful. Nor is small necessarily beautiful.

It is possible for a church to put on too much weight. Not all growth is good growth. The weeds in the parable of the wheat and the tares represent unwanted growth. The seeds which fell on rocky ground and those which fell upon thorns in the parable of the sower produced growth which did not last. A fig tree was cursed because it produced nothing but leaves. Nonbearing branches of the vine are to be cut off and burned.[31]

Would extension growth be better than expansion growth for some of the superchurches? Are some of the superchurches building their own kingdom rather than the kingdom of God? Is it possible to use the homogeneous unit principle as a cover for racism, classism, sexism, ageism, and so forth? What about the superchurch which becomes its own denomination? Church growth should do nothing to perpetuate segregated, segmented, and separated churches.

Church growth advocates also tend to fantasize about the role of pastors. A problem which that creates for Baptists relates to the way they play down congregational involvement in shaping policy and governing the church. Some church growth leaders want to give the preacher a carte blanche and in some churches the preacher becomes a dictator. That does not set well with Baptists who are accustomed to a congregational form of church government.

Fogism. There is considerable fog in church growth. Some new terminology is unnecessary baggage. Such is the case with Eurica (equal Europe plus North America), Afericasia (equal Africa plus Asia), Latfricasia (equal Latin America, Africa, Asia), and so on.

This fogism also expresses itself in overstatements which result in overkill. For example, the statements about church growth principles being worldwide truths, and the contention that churches which are not growing are out of the will of God. If ethnikitis and old age are terminal diseases, then certain kinds of church growth cannot occur in churches afflicted with those diseases. Such overstatements unnecessarily arouse the anxiety of some faithful pastors of such churches.

Until church growth is thoroughly integrated into the warp and woof of our congregational and denominational life, and until a more wholistic approach is made by its theoreticians, it will remain a potential battlefield as well as a potential gold mine.

Epilogue: The Church Growth Which We Seek

What shall we say about this cacophony of sounds concerning church growth? How can we make sense out of this voluminous, and frequently conflicting, material on church growth?

I should like to make three simple suggestions which may enable us to maneuver safely—and I also trust more swiftly—through the river of church growth.

The church growth which we seek should be *biblical.* By biblical, I do not mean that we should find a proof text for everything we attempt in church growth. I mean we ought to seek church growth which has its genesis, basis, and guidelines in the Bible. We ought to diligently search what the Scriptures have to say about church growth.

An example of the biblical base which we should seek may be found in Genesis 15:5-6 and in Ephesians 4:4-16. Look again at the Genesis passage. There God promised Abraham that his descendants will be as numerous as the stars. Elsewhere God promised Jacob that his descendants will be as numerous as the dust of the earth (Gen. 28:14) and as the sand of the sea (32:12). Paul in Romans applies the promise of Genesis to the church— even to the Gentiles—and calls Abraham "the father of us all" (compare Rom. 4:13-25). In Galatians Paul quotes the Genesis 15 passage and goes so far as to say that the gospel was preached to Abraham at that point (compare Gal. 3:6-9)!

We may conclude from all of this that God may be more concerned with numbers than are we. Certainly, if God wants his church to be as numerous as the stars of the heavens, the sand of the seas, and the dust particles of the earth, there is still much room for growth.

Now, look once more at the Ephesians passage. Note the phrases "bodily growth," "mature manhood," and "grow up in every way into him who is the head, into Christ." This is a passage on the church. To Paul, church growth is "bodily growth" because the church is the body of Christ. Also, to Paul, Jesus Christ is the perfect model for measuring "mature manhood."

The church growth which we seek should be *balanced*. It should exhibit balance between quantity and quality, between ingrowth and outgrowth, between pragmatics and ethics.

There need not be any conflict between quantity and quality. Conflict arises between the two only when either one is magnified out of proportion to the other. Advocates of church growth who pitch their tent in the book of Numbers need to move on to the prophets, the Gospels, and the Epistles. On the other hand, those advocates of church growth who insistently cry out, "Give me quality," need to be reminded that the book of Numbers is one of the sixty-six canonical books of the Holy Bible.

Churches grow through both ingrowth and outgrowth. Some folk call ingrowth biological growth and outgrowth conversion growth. Ingrowth, or biological growth, is growth from within. Outgrowth, or conversion growth, is growth from without. One is growth through inreach. The other is growth through outreach.

The church which grows only through reaching its own children, or its own kind, is incestuous. But, the church which grows only through reaching outsiders neglects Christian nurture.

Churches grow through using pragmatic *and* ethical methods. We must ask of every church growth method: "Does it work?" But, before we ask that pragmatic question, we should ask the ethical question: "Is it right?" If we ask only the pragmatic question, we may end up playing the numbers game. The church caught up in her own numbers racket is a pathetic sight! On the other hand, if we ask only the ethical question, we may end up committing institutional suicide. The church with no converts to count is no count!

The church growth which we seek should be *bullish*. Remember the television advertisement with a big bull and the line: "Merrill, Lynch, Fenner and Pierce is bullish on America"? Well, we ought to be bullish on church growth. The term, of course, belongs to the stock market. A bearish market is uncertain, shaky, and withdrawn like the bear who goes into hibernation for the long, cold winter; whereas, a bullish market is strong, confident of the future, and moving forward with a full head of steam. Both terms have to do with attitude.

I am suggesting that we ought to have a bullish attitude about church growth. We ought to be positive and excited about the future of the church. Dr. McGavran has well said: "We are in the sunrise, not the sunset of missions." Opportunity blazes today as bright as the noonday sun. According to Dr. Kenneth Scott Latourette, the nineteenth century was "the great century" in missions. But, according to Donald McGavran, the twentieth century may well be "the greatest century."

Some years ago an interesting radio program amplified a variety of sounds several times beyond their normal volume. One of the sounds was that of a precision watch, claimed by the announcer to be "the world's most perfect time piece." The watch ticked away: "click-clack, click-clack, click-clack." Later in the program, the announcer said: "Now we want you to listen to the heartbeat of the world's champion mile-runner, Bob Mathias." There followed a steady throb: "lub-dub, lub-dub, lubdub." The sound of the "click-clack" and "lub-dub" may help us to know the difference between a bearish church and a bullish church. The bearish church is an organization put together by man, which like the watch goes "click-clack." The bullish church is an organism put together by the Holy Spirit, which like the heart of Bob Mathias goes "lub-dub." We can be bullish about church growth because the church is a "lub-dub" and not a "click-clack."[1]

Notes

Chapter 1

1. C. Peter Wagner, *Your Church Can Grow* (Glendale, Ca.: Regal, 1976), p. 170.

2. Ibid., p. 12.

3. But, see C. Peter Wagner, " 'Church Growth': More Than a Man, a Magazine, a School, a Book," *Christianity Today* (XVIII, No. 5, December 7, 1973), pp. 11, 12, 14. Hereafter, this will be cited as Wagner, "More Than a Man."

4. A. R. Tippett, ed., *God, Man and Church Growth* (Grand Rapids: Wm. B. Eerdmans Publishing Co., 1973), pp. 1-46.

5. Ibid., pp. 5-12.

6. See *Evangelism,* Tambaram, Madras Series, Volume III. (London: Oxford University Press, 1939), pp. 63-86.

7. *God, Man and Church Growth,* p. 7.

8. *Church Growth and Group Conversion* (South Pasadena, Ca.: William Carey Library, 1973 ed.).

9. See Tippett, *God, Man and Church Growth,* pp. 19-25.

10. Ibid., pp. vii, ix.

11. The bulletin is published by Overseas Crusades, Inc., Box 66, Santa Clara, Ca. 95050. The first ten years have been collected and published in two separate volumes as follows: Donald A. McGavran, ed., *Church Growth Bulletin,* Vols. I-V (South Pasadena, Ca.: William Carey Library, 1969); and Donald A. McGavran, ed., *Church Growth Bulletin,* Second Consolidated Volume, September 1969 to July 1975 (South Pasadena, Ca.: William Carey Library, 1977). As of volume XVII, No. 1, January-February, 1980, the name of the *Church Growth Bulletin* was changed to *Global Church Growth Bulletin.*

12. Wagner, *Your Church Can Grow,* pp. 17, 18, 20. See also *Church Growth Bulletin,* Second Consolidated Volume, pp. 78-79. Note that MARC was founded as a joint project with the School of World Mission, Fuller Theological Seminary, and continues to work closely with that school. The Center is dedicated to undergirding the task of Christ's church by providing a

strategic information center on the work of the church world-wide, by applying a management systems approach to the task of missions at home and abroad, and by doing cooperative research in evangelism and church growth.

13. The *Global Church Growth Bulletin* (Vol. XVII, No. 2, March-April, 1980), p. 25, announced a forthcoming revised edition of this book.

14. Quoted in *Church Growth Bulletin,* Second Consolidated Volume, p. 98.

15. Wagner, *Your Church Can Grow,* p. 14.

Chapter 2

1. Both papers were published by the Lausanne Committee for World Evangelization in 1978, and are available from the committee at P.O. Box 1100, Wheaton, Ill. 60187. Five of the ten participants in the Pasadena Consultation were, or had been, faculty members of Fuller School of World Mission. Two of the twenty-eight participants in the Willowbank Consultation were from Fuller.

2. See C. Peter Wagner, *Your Church Can Be Healthy* (Nashville: Abingdon, 1978), p. 70.

3. "COCU: Moving 'with All Due Reverent Speed,' " *The Christian Century,* XCVI, No. 11, March 28, 1979, pp. 331-332.

4. Elmer L. Towns, *Is the Day of the Denomination Dead?* (Nashville: Thomas Nelson, Inc., 1973), pp. 26, 131-147.

5. Elmer L. Towns, *The Ten Largest Sunday Schools and What Makes Them Grow* (Grand Rapids: Baker Book House, 1969), pp. 5-6.

6. See Towns, *Is the Day of the Denomination Dead?* p. 24: "Today super-aggressive churches are starting colleges and seminaries at the rate of one a week. Recently the author made a list of 61 colleges founded in the last two years in independent churches."

7. See ibid., p. 18, where W. A. Criswell is quoted as saying: "Our church doesn't need the Southern Baptist Convention, they need us." Compare also p. 136: "The super aggressive church has eliminated many of the reasons for a denomination."

8. Calvin Miller, *A View from the Fields* (Nashville: Broadman, 1978), p. 22.

9. See Bishop Wood's chapter, "Lay Training for Evangelism," in Sherwood Eliot Wirt, ed., *Evangelism the Next Ten Years* (Waco: Word Books, 1978), p. 90.

10. See Alfred C. Krass, "What the Mainline Denominations Are Doing in Evangelism," *The Christian Century,* XCVI, No. 16, May 2, 1979, pp. 490-496.

11. See *Evangelism,* Vol. III, op. cit., p. 425.

12. Ibid., p. 415.

13. See Walter Houston Clark, *The Oxford Group: Its History and Significance* (New York: Bookman Associates, 1951). Clark says: "The Oxford Group from its very beginning has self-consciously striven to be non-professional or lay in its emphasis" (p. 25).

14. I refer to Hendrick Kraemer's, *A Theology of the Laity* (Philadelphia: The Westminster Press, 1958).

15. See Irving Harris, *The Breeze of the Spirit: Sam Shoemaker and the Story of Faith-at-Work* (New York: The Seabury Press, 1978).

16. The best treatment of the Keswick Movement I know is to be found in Lewis A. Drummond's, *The Awakening that Must Come* (Nashville: Broadman Press, 1978), pp. 45-64, chap. 4, "Filled, Satisfied, Victorious, and Useful."

Chapter 3

1. See Wagner, *Your Church Can Grow,* pp. 13-14.

2. Ibid., p. 14.

3. Ibid., p. 15.

4. Paul Benjamin, *The Growing Congregation* (Lincoln, Ill.: Lincoln Christian College Press, 1972). Benjamin also authored a *Workbook/Study Guide* to accompany his book. It is by the same publisher in 1972.

5. Wagner, *Your Church Can Grow,* p. 17.

6. Donald Anderson McGavran, *The Bridges of God* (New York: Friendship Press, 1955).

7. Donald A. McGavran and Win C. Arn, *How to Grow a Church* (Glendale, Ca.: Regal, 1973).

8. McGavran, *The Bridges of God,* p. 68.

9. McGavran and Arn, *How to Grow a Church,* no page number. Italics are mine.

10. Part of this data is based on Wagner's, *Your Church Can Grow,* p. 17.

11. Dean M. Kelley, *Why Conservative Churches Are Growing* (New York: Harper and Row, Publishers, 1972). A new and updated paperback edition was published in 1977.

12. See Wagner, *Your Church Can Grow,* p. 15.

13. Vergil Gerber, *A Manual for Evangelism/Church Growth*

(South Pasadena, Ca.: William Carey Library, 1973). The manual was jointly published in a 1974 edition by the same publisher and by Regal under the new title of *God's Way to Keep a Church Going and Growing*.

14. Ibid., p. 8.

15. Ebbie C. Smith, *A Manual for Church Growth Surveys* (South Pasadena, Ca.: William Carey Library, 1976).

16. Charles L. Chaney and Ron S. Lewis, *Manual for Design for Church Growth* (Nashville: Broadman Press, 1977). This manual was published in late 1977, whereas Gerber's was done in early 1973.

Chapter 4

1. See C. Peter Wagner, "Plan Rosario: Milepost for Saturation Evangelism," *Church Growth Bulletin* 14 (September 1977): 145-149.

2. This is based on my personal notes from a lecture by Dr. McGavran on 10/13/78 at Bethel Seminary in St. Paul, Minnesota.

3. Willis is now employed by The Sunday School Board of the Southern Baptist Convention in Nashville, and Smith is teaching at Southwestern Baptist Theological Seminary in Fort Worth. The study by Willis is exceedingly well done and deserves to be used as a model for comparable research.

4. See "Nazarenes 'Get Ready to Grow,' " *Church Growth Bulletin* 14 (May 1978): 203-204.

5. See *Church Growth: America* 4 (March-April 1978): 8-9.

6. Dr. Benjamin's organization may be reached at P.O. Box 3760, Washington, D.C. 20007, or 8301 Greensboro Drive, McLean, Virginia 22101.

7. See Wagner, *Your Church Can Grow,* p. 17. Oliver has now left the Canadian Church Growth Center.

8. Information taken from my personal notes on Dr. McGavran's lecture 10/13/78 at Bethel Seminary in St. Paul, Minnesota.

9. See Lyle E. Schaller, "Evaluating the Potential for Growth"; C. Peter Wagner, "The Cost of Church Growth"; J. Eugene Wright, "Church Growth: Ultimate or Penultimate?"; and James Armstrong, "The Right Kind of Church Growth"; *The Christian Ministry* 10 (January 1979): 5-17.

10. See *Vine Life: The Journal of Pastoring* 1 (March 1979).

11. Carl S. Dudley, "Measuring Church Growth," *The Christian Century* 96 (June 6-13, 1979): 635-639.

12. Donald A. McGavran and Win Arn, *Ten Steps for Church Growth* (New York: Harper and Row, Publishers, 1977).

13. The seven titles are M. Wendell Belew, *Churches and How They Grow* (1971); C. B. Hogue, *I Want My Church to Grow* (1977); Charles L. Chaney and Ron S. Lewis, *Design for Church Growth* (1977) and *Manual for Design for Church Growth* (1977); Francis M. DuBose, *How Churches Grow in an Urban World* (1978); Calvin Miller, *A View from the Fields* (1978); and Jack Redford, *Planting New Churches* (1978).

14. DuBose offers the most critical critique. Chaney and Lewis were the first Broadman authors to dialogue with the church growth movement. Miller wrestles with the church growth point of view, but is not uncritical.

15. See Wagner, *Your Church Can Grow,* pp. 19-20.

16. Originally entitled, *How Biblical Is the Church Growth Movement?*

17. Taken from my personal notes on a public telephone dialogue with Dr. McGavran in Nashville, 4/17/78.

18. "Planting Churches: The Calculated Approach," *Christianity Today* 23 (Jan. 19, 1979):8. See also Howard G. Hageman, "The Reformed Churches: Enlarging Their Witness," *The Christian Century* 96 (February 21, 1979): 178.

19. See Jean Caffey Lyles, "Should Methodists Buy the 'Church Growth' Package?" *The Christian Century* 94 (Dec. 28, 1977): 1214-1215. Also, see the response of readers under the heading, "The Real Meaning of Church Growth," *The Christian Century* 95 (March 8, 1978): 242, 244, 246. See also the editorial, "From the Editor," *Church Growth: America* 4 (March-April 1978): 2.

20. Browne Barr, "Finding the Good at Garden Grove," *The Christian Century* 94 (May 4, 1977): 424-427. See also the letters to the editor under the heading " 'Earshot' and Beyond," *The Christian Century* 94 (August 31, September 7, 1977): 764-765.

21. See McGavran and Arn, *How to Grow a Church,* p. 49. Also, see Bruce W. Jones, "I Thought You'd Never Ask: the Adventures of Evangelistic Praying," *Church Growth: America* 5 (March-April 1979) 14-15.

22. See *Christianity Today,* Vol. XXIV, No. 12 (June 27, 1980), p. 61.

23. See *Christianity Today,* Vol. XXIV, No. 10 (May 23, 1980), pp. 42-43.

Chapter 5

1. See James E. Carter, "Outreach Theology: A Comparison of Southern Baptist Thought and the Church Growth Movement," *Baptist History and Heritage,* Vol. XV, No. 3 (July 1980), p. 33.

2. Ibid., p. 33.

3. William Preston Clemmons, *The Development of a Sunday School Strategy in the Southern Baptist Convention, 1896-1926,* p. 217. Unpublished 1971 Ed.D. thesis at Southern Baptist Theological Seminary, Louisville, Ky.

4. See ibid., pp. 146, 168, 207.

5. Ibid., p. 215.

6. Quoted by Clemmons, pp. 204-205. The revised edition of 1954 reads: "The supreme business of Christianity is to win the lost to Christ." See Arthur Flake, *Building a Standard Sunday School* (Nashville: Sunday School Board of the Southern Baptist Convention, 1954 rev. ed.), p. 98.

7. Clemmons, p. 247.

8. Carter, p. 56. This may also be seen in the book by Will Beal (compiler), *The Minister of Education As a Growth Agent* (Nashville: Convention Press, 1978).

9. W. Charles Arn, ed., *Church Growth: America* (Institute for American Church Growth, March-April 1980), Vol. 6, No. 2, p. 2.

10. See Eugene Skelton's, *10 Fastest Growing Southern Baptist Sunday Schools* (Nashville: Broadman Press, 1974).

11. The Growth Section of the Sunday School Department began publishing a monthly tabloid newspaper in August 1980, called *Sunday School Growth Journal.*

12. These plans are being made for 1982-85 by the Church Growth Section of the Sunday School Department, The Sunday School Board of the Southern Baptist Convention.

13. The Baptist Press release which announced the document, "Growing Southern Baptist Churches," said: "We are drawing together on an agreement of the definition, characteristics, and principles of church growth, so that we can present a unified approach. The agreement assures that each agency is saying the same thing about growing churches. As we have a common approach, we can provide the resources which will help each church grow in its own way."

14. Elvis Marcum's *Outreach: God's Miracle Business* (Nashville: Broadman Press, 1975), is one concrete example of

what Southern Baptists can contribute to the church growth movement. C. B. Hogue's *I Want My Church to Grow* (Nashville: Broadman Press, 1977), is another example. The four "Commemorative Sunday School Classics," reissued on the 200th anniversary of Sunday Schools by The Sunday School Board of the Southern Baptist Convention, are a third example of what Southern Baptists have to contribute to the church growth movement. These volumes are: Arthur Flake's *Building a Standard Sunday School* (1954 rev. ed.); P. E. Burroughs' *How to Win to Christ* (1934); J. N. Barnette's *A Church Using Its Sunday School* (1937); and, A. V. Washburn's *Outreach for the Unreached* (1960).

Chapter 6

1. Quoted by David H. C. Read, *Go and Make Disciples* (Nashville: Abingdon, 1978), pp. 29-30.
2. Op. cit., pp. 127-130.
3. Donald A. McGavran, "When the Church Grows," quoted in J. W. Pickett, A. L. Warnshuis, G. H. Singh, and D. A. McGavran, *Church Growth and Group Conversion,* 5th ed. (South Pasadena, Ca.: William Carey Library, 1973), p. 98. Italics are mine.
4. McGavran, *Understanding Church Growth,* p. 47.
5. Louis L. King, "The New Shape," in *Crucial Issues in Missions Tomorrow,* ed., Donald A. McGavran (Chicago: Moody Press, 1972), p. 119.
6. McGavran and Arn, *Ten Steps for Church Growth,* p. 127.
7. *A View from the Fields,* p. 93.
8. Used in the film, *How to Grow a Church,* produced by the Institute for American Church Growth, and available through Christian Communication, 150 Los Robles, #600, Pasadena, Ca. 91101.
9. See Orlando E. Costas, *The Church and Its Mission: A Shattering Critique from the Third World* (Wheaton, Ill.: Tyndale House Publishers, 1974), pp. 89-90.
10. See Wagner, *Your Church Can Grow,* pp. 62-63.
11. See Vergil Gerber, *A Manual for Evangelism/Church Growth* (South Pasadena, Ca.: William Carey Library, 1973), p. 47.
12. See Charles L. Chaney and Ron S. Lewis, *Design for Church Growth* (Nashville: Broadman Press, 1977), p. 91.
13. See Wagner, *Your Church Can Grow,* pp. 63, 64.

14. See McGavran, *Church Growth Bulletin,* Second Consolidated Volume, pp. 213-214, 252, 286, 342.

15. See McGavran, *Understanding Church Growth,* p. 85.

16. Wagner, *Your Church Can Grow,* p. 110.

17. McGavran, *Church Growth Bulletin,* Vols. 1-5, p. 84.

18. The quotation is from McGavran and Arn, *Ten Steps for Church Growth,* p. 129.

19. Most of this on E-1 through E-3 comes from McGavran and Arn, *How to Grow a Church,* pp. 51-53.

20. Paul R. Orjala, *Get Ready to Grow: Principles of Church Growth* (Kansas City, Mo.: Beacon Hill Press, 1978), p. 45.

21. Ibid., p. 57. I am indebted to Orjala for the clearest explanation of EP which I have seen.

22. See the manuals cited earlier by Gerber, Smith, and Chaney and Lewis.

23. McGavran and Arn, *Ten Steps for Church Growth,* pp. 84-85, treat this law.

24. See Wagner, *Your Church Can Grow,* pp. 137-140.

25. McGavran, *Understanding Church Growth,* p. 9.

26. DuBose, *How Churches Grow in an Urban World,* p. 171.

27. McGavran, *Church Growth Bulletin,* Vols. 1-5, p. 25.

Chapter 7

1. Alan R. Tippett, *Church Growth and the Word of God* (Grand Rapids: Wm. B. Eerdmans Publishing Co., 1970), p. 9.

2. Wagner, *Your Church Can Grow* (Glendale, Ca.: Regal, 1976), p. 165.

3. McGavran, ed., *Church Growth Bulletin,* Vols. 1-5 (South Pasadena, Ca.: William Carey Library, 1979), p. 200.

4. J. Eugene Wright, "Church Growth: Ultimate or Penultimate?" *The Christian Ministry* 10 (Jan. 1979):14.

5. Tom Houston, "Evangelism and Church Growth," in *Evangelism: The Next Ten Years,* ed. Sherwood Eliot Wirt (Waco: Word Books, 1978), pp. 133-134.

Chapter 8

1. Both quotes are from Wagner, "More Than a Man," p. 12.

2. Arthur F. Glasser, "Church Growth and Theology," *God, Man and Church Growth,* p. 53.

3. Ibid., p. 54.

4. See Costas, op. cit., p. 133.

5. Ibid., p. 131.

6. Ibid., p. 132.

7. John H. Yoder, "Church Growth Issues in Theological Perspective," in *The Challenge of Church Growth,* ed., Wilbert R. Shenk (Scottsdale, Penn.: Herald Press, 1973), p. 27.

8. Glasser, in *God, Man and Church Growth,* p. 52.

9. "Intensity of Belief: a Pragmatic Concern for Church Growth," *Christianity Today* 21 (Jan. 7, 1977):10.

10. Pickett and Others, *Church Growth and Group Conversion,* p. 99.

11. McGavran, *Church Growth Bulletin,* Vols. 1-5, p. 25.

12. McGavran, *The Bridges of God,* pp. 13-15.

13. "How About That New Verb 'to Disciple'?" *Church Growth Bulletin* 15 (May 1979): 265-270, but esp. 266-267.

14. Robert L. Ramseyer, "Anthropological Perspectives on Church Growth Theory," in *The Challenge of Church Growth,* p. 69.

15. Wagner, "More Than a Man," p. 14.

16. Vol. 6 (Nov. 1977):39. Italics are McGavran's.

17. Wagner, *Your Church Can Grow,* pp. 158-59.

18. *Social Action vs. Evangelism: An Essay on the Contemporary Crises* (South Pasadena, Ca.: William Carey Library, 1977), pp. 13-39.

19. Donald McGavran, *The Clash Between Christianity and Cultures* (Washington, D.C.: Canon Press, 1974), pp. 41-42.

20. Ibid., pp. 39, 14.

21. See Ramseyer, *The Challenge of Church Growth,* p. 67.

22. McGavran, *Understanding Church Growth,* p. 161.

23. Ibid., p. 154.

24. Ibid., pp. 150-152.

25. I am indebted to Ramseyer, pp. 68, 73, for some assistance in articulating these two paragraphs.

26. Edward F. Murphy, quoted in McGavran, *Crucial Issues in Missions Tomorrow,* p. 262.

27. *Church Growth Bulletin,* Vols. 1-5, p. 84.

28. Compare Ramseyer, p. 68, and McQuilkin, pp. 50-66.

29. Wagner, *Your Church Can Be Healthy* (Nashville: Abingdon, 1979).

30. "Great Campaign Evangelism," *Crucial Issues in Missions Tomorrow,* p. 203. Italics are Peters's.

31. See Wagner, *Your Church Can Grow,* p. 140, and "More Than a Man," p. 14.

32. *Church Growth Bulletin,* Vols. 1-5, p. 178.
33. See Pickett and others, *Church Growth and Group Conversion,* p. v.
34. McGavran, *Understanding Church Growth,* p. 58.
35. See McGavran's *Crucial Issues in Missions Tomorrow,* p. 28.
36. Ralph Winter, *The 25 Unbelievable Years* (South Pasadena, Ca.: William Carey Library, 1970), p. 61.
37. See Wagner, *Your Church Can Grow,* p. 53.
38. Robert H. Schuller, *Your Church Has Real Possibilities* (Glendale, Ca.: Regal, 1974), esp. pp. 85-98, the chapter entitled, "Possibility Thinking Makes Miracles Happen."
39. McGavran, *Understanding Church Growth,* pp. 59, 213.
40. *Church Growth Bulletin,* Vols. 1-5, p. 213. Italics are McGavran's.
41. Quoted in Tippett, *God, Man and Church Growth,* p. 143.

Chapter 9
1. See McGavran and Arn, *Ten Steps for Church Growth,* p. 127.
2. See McGavran, *Understanding Church Growth,* pp. 335-353, and esp. 336.
3. Ramseyer, *The Challenge of Church Growth,* p. 67.
4. McGavran and Arn, *Ten Steps for Church Growth,* p. 126.
5. Wagner, "More Than a Man," p. 14.
6. Peter Wagner quoted these statistics in a lecture to SBC evangelism leaders in December, 1975.
7. The phrase is McGavran's in *Ten Steps for Church Growth,* p. 2.
8. I am indebted to Ron S. Lewis for putting me onto this principle.
9. See David A. Womack, *The Pyramid Principle,* pp. 139 and 80.
10. Ibid., p. 57.
11. I base this on my personal notes from a lecture by Wolf to the Advanced Church Growth Seminar for Professionals in Pasadena, California, January 1978.
12. See DuBose, *How Churches Grow in an Urban World,* pp. 169-170.
13. See Linda Lawson, "Andy Anderson Creates Action—and Now the Growth Spiral," *Facts and Trends,* 22 (July-August 1978):6-7.
14. Ibid., p. 7.

15. McGavran, *Understanding Church Growth*, p. 256.

16. See *The Contagious Congregation*, p. 104.

17. McGavran, *Understanding Church Growth*, p. 256.

18. Ibid., pp. 256-257.

19. See W. Charles Arn, "Receptivity—Rating Scale," *Church Growth: America* 4 (Summer 1978):3.

20. The above paragraphs are based on the above article by Charles Arn.

21. See the *MARC Newsletter* (Monrovia, Ca.: Missions Advanced Research and Communication Center, Nov. 1977), pp. 6, 8.

22. DuBose, *How Churches Grow in an Urban World*, p. 170.

23. See Costas, p. 146.

24. I refer to James F. Engle and H. Wilbert Norton, *What's Gone Wrong with the Harvest?* (Grand Rapids: Zondervan Publishing House, 1975).

25. Ibid., p. 45. Compare with James F. Engle, "Accountability for World Evangelization," *Church Growth Bulletin,* Second Consolidated Volume, p. 333.

26. I base these remarks on my personal copy of Neighbor's model and on a lecture which he gave in San Francisco, California during December of 1978.

27. See Chaney and Lewis, *Design for Church Growth,* pp. 33, 61-63.

28. Ibid., p. 33.

29. See Richard A. Myers, "Sunday School, Small Groups and Church Growth," *Church Growth: America* 4 (Sept.-Oct. 1978):8-9.

30. *Understanding Church Growth*, p. 198.

31. *Ten Steps for Church Growth*, p. 129.

32. McGavran and Arn, *How to Grow a Church*, p. 45. See also pp. 44-45.

33. See "Should the Church Be a Melting Pot?" *Christianity Today* 22 (Aug. 18, 1978):10-16.

34. *Get Ready to Grow*, p. 63.

35. DuBose, *How Churches Grow in an Urban World*, p. 126. See also pp. 121-134, 170.

36. See Orjala, *Get Ready to Grow*, pp. 62-64.

37. See McGavran's *Understanding Church Growth*, p. 183.

38. Some of these statistics are taken from *Missions Update* (Atlanta: Home Mission Board Missions Section, March 28, 1979).

39. See *Your Church Can Grow*, pp. 122-123. See also

"Should the Church Be a Melting Pot?" *Christianity Today,* p. 12. John Knox Press came out with a new book by Peter Wagner in 1979, entitled *Our Kind of People.* Wagner deals in that manuscript with the ethical implications of the HU principle.

40. Alan R. Tippett, "The Holy Spirit and Responsive Populations," in McGavran's *Crucial Issues in Missions Tomorrow,* pp. 84-85.

41. Lyle E. Schaller, "Evaluating the Potential for Growth," *The Christian Ministry* 10 (Jan. 1979):7.

42. See Vol. 48, p. 12.

43. Wagner, *Your Church Can Grow,* p. 61.

44. It is interesting to note that many denominations and judicatories now have more class five leaders than ever before. Yet, they are growing at a slower rate than when they had fewer such leaders, or no such leaders.

45. Lewis shared these in a seminar on church growth at Midwestern Baptist Theological Seminary, Kansas City, Missouri, during January 1979.

46. See Robert H. Schuller, *Your Church Has Real Possibilities* (Glendale, Ca.: Regal, 1974), pp. 19-20.

47. McGavran and Arn, *Ten Steps for Church Growth,* p. 129.

48. See F. D. Brumer, *A Theology of the Holy Spirit* (Grand Rapids: Wm. B. Eerdmans, 1970), p. 43.

49. *Your Spiritual Gifts Can Help Your Church Grow* (Glendale, Ca.: Regal, 1979).

50. See C. Peter Wagner, "The Myth of the Church Growth Pastor," *Church Growth America* 4 (Sept.-Oct. 1978):4-5, 12-15.

51. Ibid., p. 13.

52. See Wagner, *Your Church Can Grow,* pp. 75-83. I am also basing some of this on my personal notes from a lecture by Wagner to the Advanced Church Growth Seminar for Professionals in Pasadena, California during January of 1978.

53. See Wagner, *Your Church Can Grow,* pp. 69-82.

Chapter 10

1. I am indebted to Lyle Schaller for this idea. It is based on my notes of a lecture by Schaller in January 1978, in Pasadena, California.

2. *Church Growth Bulletin,* Vols. 1-5, p. 30.

3. Ibid., p. 69.

4. See Peter Mankres, "Small Is Beautiful: Churches As if People Mattered," *The Christian Century* 95 (May 1978): 492-493.

5. See Robert K. Hudnut, *Church Growth Is Not the Point* (New York: Harper and Row, Publishers, 1975), pp. ix, xi, and 32.

6. See Wendell Belew, "America Needs More Churches," *Church Growth: America,* Vol. I, No. 4, 1-2 and 7. See also, *Missions Update* (March 28, 1979) published by Home Mission Board's Missions Section, Atlanta, Georgia.

7. See C. Peter Wagner, "How 'Christian' Is America?" *Christianity Today* 21 (December 3, 1976):14.

8. See Carl S. Dudley, "Measuring Church Growth," *The Christian Century* 96 (June 6-13, 1979):638.

9. *The Unfinished Reformation* (New York: Harper & Brothers, 1953). See esp. pp. 26-47.

10. (Nashville: Thomas Nelson, Inc., 1973).

11. The phrase is mine, but I am indebted to Lyle Schaller for suggesting the idea.

12. Edward R. Dayton, "Disciplined Planning and Data Retrieval," *God, Man and Church Growth,* p. 423.

13. Ibid., p. 421.

14. See Charles G. Finney, *Reflections on Revival,* comp. by Donald W. Dayton (Minneapolis, Minn.: Bethany Fellowship Inc., 1979), esp. pp. 113-119. Cf. also Donald W. Dayton, *Discovering an Evangelical Heritage* (New York: Harper and Row, 1976).

15. David Haney, *The Lord and His Laity* (Nashville: Broadman Press, 1978), pp. 20-21.

16. *Church Growth Bulletin,* Vols. 1-5, p. 73.

17. See Melvin L. Hodges, "Surmounting Seven Obstacles to Church Growth," *Church Growth Bulletin,* 2nd Consolidated Volume, p. 44.

18. See George W. Peters, *Saturation Evangelism* (Grand Rapids: Zondervan, 1970), p. 53.

19. John T. Seamands, "The Role of the Holy Spirit in Church Growth," *God, Man and Church Growth,* p. 103.

20. I am quoting from my notes on a lecture by Schaller in Pasadena, California during January of 1978.

21. See Lyle E. Schaller, "Evaluating the Potential for Growth," *The Christian Ministry* 10 (Jan. 1979):7.

22. See C. Peter Wagner, *Your Church Can Be Healthy* (Nashville: Abingdon, 1979).

23. See C. Peter Wagner, "The Pathology of Church Growth," *Theology, News and Notes* (October 1977), published by Fuller Theological Seminary, Pasadena, California.

The paragraphs which follow are also based on this article. See pp. 5-9, 38.

24. *Church Growth Bulletin,* 2nd Consolidated Volume, p. 44.

Chapter 11

1. "Evangelism and Church Growth," in *Evangelism the Next Ten Years,* p. 133.

2. McGavran and Arn, *Ten Steps for Church Growth,* p. 51.

3. See Donald A. McGavran, "The Dimensions of World Evangelization," in J. D. Douglas, ed., *Let the Earth Hear His Voice* (Minneapolis, Minnesota: World Wide Publications, 1975), pp. 104-108. See also, "What About That Two Billion?—Part II," in the *MARC Newsletter* (November, 1974), for a lucid discussion of these symbols. This fourfold typology has been refined into a sevenfold typology by George G. Hunter in "HUP Clarifies Evangelism," *Global Church Growth Bulletin,* Vol. XVII, No. 2, March-April, 1980, pp. 24-25.

4. See John R. W. Stott, "Gospel and Culture," *Christianity Today* (April 7, 1978), pp. 42-43.

5. See *Lausanne Occasional Papers,* No. 2, The Willowbank Report—Gospel and Culture, 1978, p. 7, Lausanne Committee for World Evangelization, P.O. Box 1100, Wheaton, Illinois 60187.

6. McGavran, *Understanding Church Growth,* p. 85.

7. Quoted in *Lausanne Occasional Papers,* No. 1, The Pasadena Consultation—Homogeneous Unit, p. 3.

8. See Orjala, p. 67.

9. See Tetsuao Yamamori, "Reaching Ethnic America: Six Strategic Models," *Church Growth: America* (Vol. 4, No. 2, Nov.-Dec., 1978), pp. 4-6, 14-15.

10. *Church Growth Bulletin,* Vols. I-V, pp. 344, 306, 58f., 106, 107; see also *Understanding Church Growth,* p. 302 f., and Costas, pp. 109-111.

11. See McGavran, *The Bridges of God.*

12. See Michael Green, *Evangelism in the Early Church* (Grand Rapids: Wm. B. Eerdmans Publishing Co., 1970) pp. 207-223. Wolf lectures on the subject at church growth meetings.

13. I am indebted to Dr. McGavran for the term. See *Church Growth Bulletin,* Vols. I-V, pp. 55, 61, 84, and esp. 106-107.

14. "Mass Evangelism: the Bottom Line," *Church Growth: America* (Vol. 4, No. 1, January-February, 1978), p. 18.

15. I am relating this from my memory, based on a cassette by Peter Wagner in December, 1975.

16. See Womack, p. 139.

17. (Regal, 1979).

18. Wagner, *Your Church Can Grow,* pp. 75-83.

19. Ibid., p. 72.

20. Ibid., p. 74.

21. Ibid., pp. 139-140. See also Gerber's *God's Way to Keep a Church Going and Growing.*

22. For a different approach see Wagner's "How to Diagnose the Health of Your Church," *Christianity Today* (Vol. XVII, No. 8, Jan. 19, 1973), pp. 24-25.

23. "The Pathology of Church Growth," *Theology, News and Notes,* pp. 5-9, 38.

24. McGavran, *Understanding Church Growth,* p. 58.

25. *Church Growth Bulletin,* Vol. I-V, p. 213.

26. "Disciplined Planning and Data Retrieval," in *God, Man and Church Growth,* p. 423.

27. *Church Growth Bulletin,* Second Consolidated Volume, p. 53.

28. Quoted by Orjala, p. 23.

29. "Mass Evangelism: the Bottom Line," pp. 4-7, 16-18.

30. "A Church Growth Look at Here's Life America," *Church Growth: America* (January-February, 1977), pp. 4-7, 9, 14-15, 27, 30.

31. "Who Found It?" (Sept. 1977), pp. 13-18.

32. (South Pasadena, Ca.: William Carey Library, 1974). See also *Your Church Can Grow,* p. 121.

33. See *Ten Steps for Church Growth,* p. 128.

34. Ibid., p. 128.

35. Ibid., pp. 127-128.

36. See Costas, pp. 89-90.

37. Based on my personal notes from a lecture by Ron Lewis in Nashville on 4/17/78.

Chapter 12

1. See "Should the Church Be a Melting Pot?" *Christianity Today* 22 (August 18, 1978):12-13.

2. See ibid., p. 14.

3. See McGavran, *Understanding Church Growth,* p. 348.

4. See Wagner, *Your Church Can Grow,* p. 168.

5. DuBose, *How Churches Grow in an Urban World,* p. 127.

6. By "critical," I do not mean *skeptical* or *liberal.* Rather, I

mean essentially what Bernard Ramm means when he discusses the critical system of hermeneutics in *Protestant Biblical Interpretation* (Boston: W. A. Wilde Co., 1950), pp. 48-77, and esp. pp. 59-61. "The critical approach stands in definite opposition to all approaches based on *arbitrariness, dogmatism,* or *imagination*" (p. 60, italics are Ramm's). The critical approach means that "any interpretation of Holy Scripture must have its *reasons.*" Every interpretation must be justified. That justification may be *historical, philological,* or *theological* (pp. 59-60).

7. *The Clash Between Christianity and Cultures,* p. 53. See also pp. 51-55. Italics are mine.

8. Ibid., pp. 56, 66.

9. Ibid., p. 41.

10. See Chaney and Lewis, *Design for Church Growth,* p. 7.

11. Alan R. Tippett, *Church Growth and the Word of God* (Grand Rapids: Wm. B. Eerdmans Publishing Company, 1970).

12. Based on a tape done by Wagner in December, 1975, and my memory of his lecture in Pasadena during the first full week in January, 1978.

13. Quoted in *The Church and Its Mission: A Shattering Critique from the Third World,* p. 137.

14. See *Church Growth Bulletin,* Second Consolidated Volume, pp. 73-84.

15. See David O. Morberg, *The Great Reversal: Evangelism and Social Concern* (Philadelphia: J. B. Lippincott Co., 1972), p. 30. A 1977 revised edition in paperback by Lippincott is also available.

16. Ibid., pp. 179, 152.

17. Wagner, *Your Church Can Grow,* p. 158.

18. "The Pros and Cons of Robert Schuller," *The Christian Century* (August 20-27, 1975): 734.

19. See Harvie M. Conn, ed., *Theological Perspectives on Church Growth* (Nutley, New Jersey: Presbyterian and Reformed Publishing Co., 1976), p. 79.

20. *The Challenge of Church Growth,* p. 28.

21. *The Church and Its Mission,* p. 135.

22. *The Clash Between Christianity and Cultures,* p. 41.

23. "How about That New Verb 'to Disciple'?" *Church Growth Bulletin* 15 (May 1979): 265-270.

24. McGavran, *The Bridges of God,* p. 14.

25. *The Challenge of Church Growth,* pp. 68-69.

26. A twelve-page paper by Hosea Bilyeu in 451G during term five, 1979.

27. See Wagner, *Your Church Can Grow.* This is Wagner's subtitle.

28. McGavran and Arn, *Ten Steps for Church Growth.*

29. Based on my notes of a lecture by McGavran on 10/3/78 at Bethel Seminary in St. Paul, Minnesota.

30. See Wagner, *Your Church Can Grow,* pp. 97-109.

31. See Tom Houston, "Evangelism and Church Growth," in *Evangelism the Next Ten Years,* pp. 133-134. See also DuBose, *How Churches Grow in an Urban World,* pp. 121-22.

Epilogue

1. Related by John T. Seamands, "The Role of the Holy Spirit in Church Growth," *God, Man and Church Growth,* pp. 95-96.